Spotlight on the USA

Randee Falk

Oxford University Press

Oxford University Press

200 Madison Avenue
New York, NY 10016 USA

Walton Street
Oxford OX2 6DP England

Library of Congress Cataloging-in-Publication Data

Falk, Randee.
  Spotlight on the USA / Randee Falk.
      p.   cm.
  ISBN 0-19-434235-2
  1. United States—Civilization. 2. United States—Geography.
  I. Title.
  E169.1.F168 1993
  973-dc20

ISBN 0-19-434235-2

Editorial Manager: Susan Lanzano
Development: Karen Davy
Editor: Paul Phillips
Designer: M. Chandler Martylewski
Art Buyer: Karen Polyak
Photo Research: Paul Hahn
Production Manager: Abram Hall

Illustrations by Pat and Robin DeWitt, Maj Britt-Hagsted, David McCall Johnson,
Joe LeMonnier, Marybeth Farrell Rothman, Kirsten Soderlind, Dahl Taylor

Realia by Stephan Van Litsenborg

Printing (last digit): 10 9 8 7 6 5 4 3 2

Printed in Hong Kong

Contents

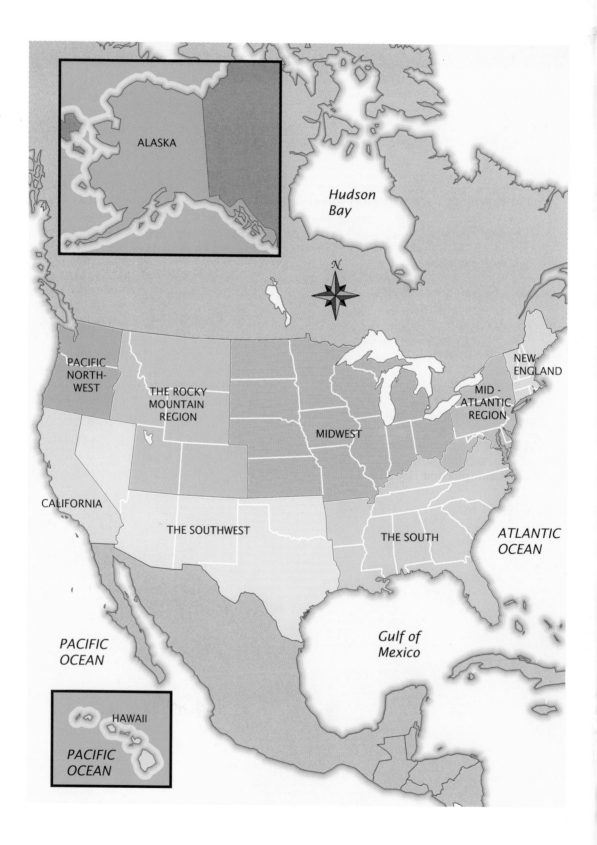

The American People

The United States has the third-largest population in the world (after China and India). In 1990, population in the United States passed the 250,000,000 mark. Who are the American people?

The most distinctive characteristic of the United States is its people. As nineteenth-century poet Walt Whitman said, the United States "is not merely a nation but a nation of nations." People from around the world have come to the United States and influenced its history and culture.

The Native Americans

The first people on the American continent came from Asia. They came across the Bering Strait from Siberia to Alaska at various times when the sea level dropped. The first migration might have been as early as 40,000 years ago. Once in America, these people migrated east across North America and south through Central and South America. When Columbus arrived in the fifteenth century, there were perhaps 10 million people in North America alone. They had developed many different kinds of societies. These were the people that Columbus called "Indians," in the mistaken belief that he had reached the East Indies.

The story of the westward growth of the United States was also the story of the destruction of the Native Americans, or Indians. Today there are about 1.5 million Indians in the United States. Western states—especially California, Oklahoma, Arizona, and New Mexico—have the largest Indian populations. About one-third of the Native Americans live on reservations, land that was set aside for them. Most of the others live in cities. Poverty and unemployment are major problems, especially on the reservations.

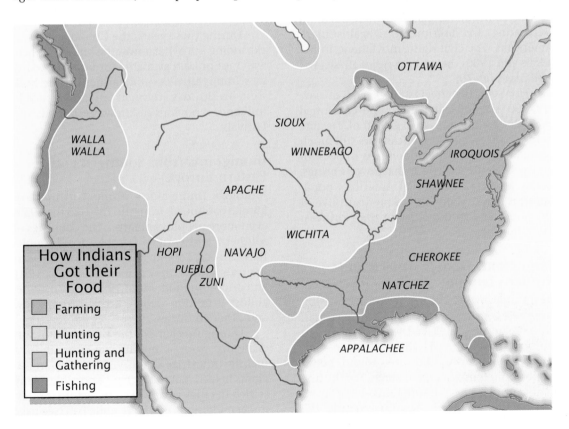

How Indians Got their Food

- Farming
- Hunting
- Hunting and Gathering
- Fishing

The British

Beginning in the 1600s, the British settled the eastern part of North America. By the time of the American Revolution (1776), the culture of the American colonists (their religion, language, government, etc.) was thoroughly British—with an American "twist." In a sense, then, the British culture was the foundation on which America was built. Also, over the years, many immigrants to the United States have come from the United Kingdom and Ireland.

African-Americans

From 1620 to 1820 by far the largest group of people to come to the United States came, not as willing immigrants, but against their will. These people were West Africans brought to work as slaves, especially on the plantations, or large farms, of the South. In all, about 8 million people were brought from Africa.

The Civil War, in the 1860s, ended slavery and established equal rights for black Americans (see pages 66–68). But many states, especially in the South, passed laws segregating (separating) and discriminating against black Americans. The civil rights movement, in the 1950s and 1960s, helped get rid of these laws (see pages 66–70).

However, the effects of 200 years of slavery, 100 years of segregation, and continued prejudice are not as easy to get rid of. Despite many changes, black Americans are still much more likely than white Americans to be poor and to suffer the bad effects that poverty brings. Today about 12 percent of America's population is black. Many black Americans live in the South and in the cities of the Northeast and Midwest.

Immigrants from Northern and Western Europe

Beginning in the 1820s, the number of immigrants coming to the United States began to increase rapidly. Faced with problems in Europe—poverty, war, discrimination—immigrants hoped for, and often found, better opportunities in the United States. For the first half-century, most immigrants were from northwestern Europe—from Germany, the United Kingdom, Ireland, Sweden, and Nor-

Immigrants arriving in the late 1800s

way. In the late 1840s, for example, widespread hunger resulting from the failure of the potato crop led many Irish people to emigrate to the United States.

During these years, the United States was expanding into what is now the Midwest. There was a lot of land available for farming. Many new immigrants became farmers in the Midwest. To this day, German and Scandinavian influence is obvious in Midwestern foods and festivals.

STUDIANR

Immigrants from Southern and Eastern Europe

Although immigration from northwestern Europe continued, from the 1870s to the 1930s even more people came from the countries of southern and eastern Europe—for example, Italy, Greece, Poland, and Russia. Like the earlier immigrants, they came to escape poverty and discrimination. From 1900 to 1910 alone, almost 9 million people arrived from these and other countries.

During this period, the United States was changing from a mainly agricultural to a mainly industrial country. The new immigrants helped make this change possible. Many settled in cities and worked in factories, often under conditions that were quite bad (see page 37).

In the 1920s discrimination and prejudice in the United States led to laws limiting immigration. Immigration slowed down until the 1960s, when these laws were changed.

Hispanic-Americans

Hispanics are people of Spanish or Spanish-American origin. Some Hispanics lived in areas that later became part of the United States (for example, in what are now the states of California and New Mexico). Many others immigrated to the United States. Hispanic immigration has increased greatly in recent decades.

Hispanics come from many different countries. Three especially large groups are Mexican-Americans (who make up about two-thirds of the total Hispanic population), Puerto Ricans, and Cuban-Americans. (Puerto Rico was a U.S. territory and since 1952 has been a self-governing commonwealth.) While the groups have much in common (especially the Spanish language), there are also many differences. The groups are also concentrated in different areas — Mexican-Americans in Texas and California, Puerto Ricans in New York, and Cuban-Americans in Florida. Many recent immigrants are from Central American countries.

Hispanics are one of the fastest growing groups in the United States population. Within 25 years, they will be the largest minority group.

Asian-Americans

In the nineteenth century, laws limited Asian immigration. Also, Asians in the United States, such as the Chinese and Japanese who had come to California, met with widespread discrimination.

Since the mid-1960s, with changes in immigration laws and with conflicts in Southeast Asia, Asians have been a major immigrant group. In the 1980s, for example, almost half of all immigrants were Asian. Countries that Asian-Americans have come from include China and Taiwan, Japan, the Philippines, Korea, Vietnam, Cambodia, Laos, Thailand, and India. Many have settled in California, Hawaii, New York, and Texas.

Melting Pots and Mosaics

For years, it was thought that the United States was and should be a "melting pot" — in other words, that people from all over the world would come and adopt the American culture as their own. More recently, some people have compared the United States to a mosaic — a picture made of many different pieces. America's strength, they argue, lies in its diversity and in the contributions made by people of many different cultures. America needs to preserve and encourage this diversity, while making sure that everyone has equal opportunity to succeed.

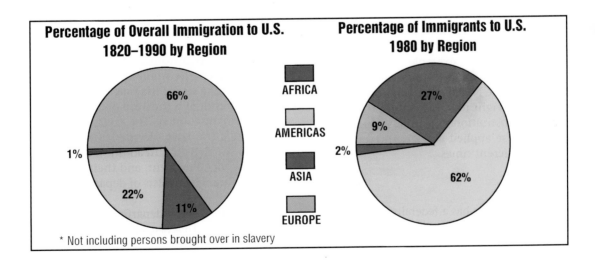

Percentage of Overall Immigration to U.S. 1820–1990 by Region

66%
1%
22%
11%

AFRICA
AMERICAS
ASIA
EUROPE

Percentage of Immigrants to U.S. 1980 by Region

27%
9%
2%
62%

* Not including persons brought over in slavery

Mosaic or melting pot?

Discussion Points
- Over the years, did many people immigrate to your country? Are there many immigrants today? Where are the immigrants from? Why did they leave their countries?
- Did many people emigrate from your country to other countries? What are some of the countries they went to? Did many people go to the United States? If so, do you know if there was a particular period when they went and a particular region where they settled?
- What do "melting pot" and "mosaic" refer to? What do you think are some of the advantages and disadvantages of each?

The Political System

The United States is an indirect democracy—that is, the people rule through representatives they elect. Over time, the vote has been given to more and more people. In the beginning, only white men with property could vote. Today any citizen who is at least 18 years old can vote.

The Constitution

The United States Constitution, written in 1787, established the country's political system and is the basis for its laws. In 200 years, the United States has experienced enormous growth and change. Yet the Constitution works as well today as when it was written. One reason is that the Constitution can be amended, or changed. (For example, the Fifteenth Amendment gave black Americans the right to vote and the Nineteenth Amendment gave women the right to vote.) Another reason is that the Constitution is flexible: its basic principles can be applied and interpreted differently at different times.

Federalism

The United States has a federalist system. This means that there are individual states, each with its own government, and there is a federal, or national, government. The Con-stitution gives certain powers to the federal government, other powers to the state governments, and yet other powers to both. For example, only the national government can print money, the states establish their own school systems, and both the national and the state governments can collect taxes.

Three Branches of Government

Within the national government, power is divided among three branches: the legislative, executive, and judicial branches.

The legislative branch consists of Congress, which has two parts—the House of Representatives and the Senate. Congress's main function is to make laws. There are 100 senators (two from each state) and 435 representatives (the number from each state depends on the size of the state's population).

The President is the head of the executive branch and the country. The executive branch administers the laws (decides how the laws should be carried out). In addition to the President, the Vice-President, and their staffs, the executive branch consists of departments and agencies.

There are now 14 departments, including Treasury, State, Defense, and Health and Human Services. Each department has different responsibilities. For example, the Treasury Department manages the nation's money, while the State Department helps make foreign policy. The President appoints the department heads, who together make up the President's Cabinet, or advisers. The agencies regulate specific areas. For example, the Environmental Protection Agency tries to control pollution, while the Securities and Exchange Commission regulates the stock markets.

The judicial branch interprets the laws and makes sure that new laws are in keeping with the Constitution. There are several levels of federal courts. The Supreme Court is the most important. It has nine members, who are appointed for life.

The system of checks and balances, established by the Constitution, is meant to prevent any branch from having too much power. Each branch has certain controls over the other branches. For example, Congress makes the laws but the president can veto, or reject, a law and the Supreme Court can decide a law is unconstitutional.

State and Local Government

Each state has its own constitution. Like the national government, state governments are divided into legislative, executive, and judicial branches. There are state senators and representatives and state court systems. Just as the President is the leader of the national government, each state has a governor as its leader. Below the state level of government, there are county and city governments.

Two-Party System

The United States has two main political parties—the Democratic and Republican parties. Many other smaller parties play little if any role.

Voters elect the president, as well as senators, representatives, governor, etc. A voter can choose candidates from different parties (e.g., vote for Republicans for President and vice-president and a Democrat for senator), so the President does not have to be from the party that has a majority in Congress. In recent years, in fact, voters have tended to choose Republican presidents and Democratic congresspeople.

There are *not* clear differences between the Republican and Democratic parties. In general, the Republicans tend to be more conservative and to have more support among the upper classes, while the Democrats tend to be more liberal and to have more support among the working classes and the poor.

The U.S. Congress at work (*Pamela Price/Picture Group*)

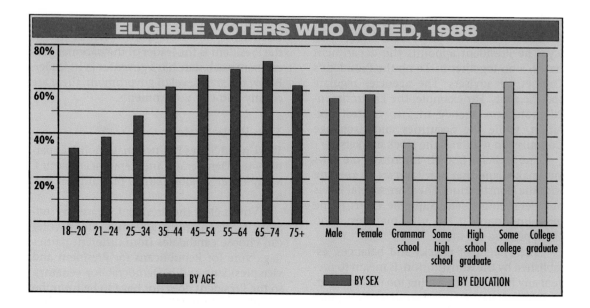

ELIGIBLE VOTERS WHO VOTED, 1988

BY AGE — BY SEX — BY EDUCATION

Recent Trends

In the twentieth century, as society has become more complex, government has taken a much more active role. However, many Americans worry about too much government interference in their lives. Still, compared to many other countries, the role of the U.S. government remains limited.

In recent years, fewer people are voting. In the 1988 presidential election, for example, only 50 percent of people of voting age actually voted. Some experts think television may have contributed to the problem. Candidates today often campaign mainly through brief TV appearances and commercials. Instead of explaining their views in detail, they try to make their opponents look bad. Understandably, in the end many voters may not feel enthusiastic about any candidate.

Discussion Points
- How many main political parties does your country have? Are there clear differences between the parties?
- What are some of the bad effects of a low voter turnout? What can be done to increase voter turnout? In your country, is voter turnout high or low?

The Economy

The Free Enterprise System

The United States economy is based on the free enterprise system: Private businesses compete against one another with relatively little interference from the government. Since the depression of the 1930s, when the economy essentially collapsed, laws have been made giving the government a more active role in economic and other matters.

Changes Over Time

Until the second half of the last century, the United States was a mainly agricultural nation. The Civil War (1861–1865) helped stimulate industry. In the years that followed, industrialization transformed the country, although many areas, especially the South, remained mainly agricultural and rural.

Agriculture and industry have been major forces in the U.S. economy.

The Situation Today

The United States is a large country and is rich in natural resources. It is a leading producer of fuel—of oil, natural gas, and coal. It is also a leading producer of many other minerals, including copper, gold, aluminum, iron, and lead. The United States grows wheat, corn, and other crops and raises many cows, pigs, and chickens.

However, the United States is also a major consumer of resources. This means, for example, that the United States must import much of the fuel it uses.

Not surprisingly, international trade is important to the United States. Major exports include machinery and high-technology equipment, chemicals, cars, aircraft, and grains. Major imports include machinery and telecommunications equipment, oil, cars, metals, and chemicals.

Today, the United States faces some major economic challenges. One important challenge is increasing its productivity, or the efficiency of the labor force, in order to increase the rate of economic growth. Another challenge, as the country shifts from manufacturing to services, is to train people to fill new kinds of jobs.

In the 1950s and 1960s, the U.S. economy grew rapidly. Many companies moved to the South and Southwest, and these areas experienced change and growth. Then, in the mid-1970s, economic growth began to slow down.

Just as there had been a shift from agriculture to industry, there is now a shift from industry to services. (Services are provided by hospitals, banks, law firms, hotels and restaurants, and so on.) In recent years, most new jobs have been service jobs.

Discussion Points
- What are some of the major imports and exports of your country?
- The passage says that in the United States two major economic challenges are (1) increasing productivity of workers and (2) training workers for new kinds of jobs. Do you know what major economic challenges your country is facing now?

Religion

Separation of Church and State

A basic American principle is separation of church (religion) and state (government). The U.S. Constitution says that people have the right to worship as they choose and that no religion can be made the official religion. In keeping with this principle, government money cannot be used to support church activities and prayers may not be said in public schools. (The U.S. Congress, however, opens each year with a prayer.)

The Different Religions

Studies show that about 9 in 10 Americans identify with a religion and that about 6 in 10 belong to a church.

About 94 percent of Americans who identify with a religion are Christians. Among Christians, there are more Protestants than Catholics. However, there are many different Protestant denominations, or groups. For example, Protestants include, among others, Baptists, Methodists, and Lutherans, and each of these groups is divided into smaller groups. So Catholics, although outnumbered by Protestants, are the single largest religious group.

Jews are the largest non-Christian group, with about 4 percent of the population. About 2 percent of the population is Moslem, and smaller numbers are Buddhists and Hindus. Native Americans often preserve their tribal religions.

Regional Differences

There are some differences among the regions when it comes to religion. In part these differences are related to where different immigrant groups settled. For example, the Lutheran religion was strong among Germans and Scandinavians. Many Germans and Scandinavians settled in the Midwest. So today there are many Lutheran churches in the Midwest.

The Baptist religion really developed in the South. Today there are still many Baptists in the Southern states. The state of Utah, in the West, was settled by Mormons. (The Mormon religion began in the United States, in the 1800s.) The majority of people in Utah today are Mormons (see page 120).

Sections of the South and, to some extent, the Midwest are sometimes called the "Bible Belt." In these areas there are many Protestant fundamentalists, who believe that the Bible is literally true and that its message should be at the center of a person's life.

Popular religious leader Billy Graham

The Family

The American family has changed greatly in the last 20 or 30 years. Many of these changes are similar to changes taking place in other countries.

Marriage and Children

Young people are waiting longer before getting married. Women are also waiting longer to have children. It's not unusual today for a

In the U.S. today, there are many different kinds of families.

woman to have her first child in her mid-thirties. And families are having fewer children. The typical family used to have three children. Today most families have one or two children.

Dual-Earning Families

In the traditional family, the wife stayed home with the children while the husband earned money. Now 60 percent of all married women work outside the home. So a majority of couples have two wage-earners. One reason for this change is that women want and expect to have careers. Another reason is economics. With rising prices, many families cannot survive on one person's salary.

Single-Parent and Other Nontraditional Families

The United States has a high divorce rate: Approximately 1 in every 2 marriages ends in divorce. One result of this high divorce rate is that many American children live in single-parent families.

Although some women wait until their thirties to have their first child, other women become mothers while they are still teenagers. Many of these teenaged mothers are not married. Many are also poor. Poverty among children in homes headed by single mothers has become a serious problem in the United States.

Often people who are divorced get married again. This has led to a new kind of family—the "reconstituted family," in which there are children from previous marriages as well as from the present marriage.

An Aging Population

In the past, it was common for three generations—grandparents, parents, and children—to live together. Now most older people live on their own. They generally stay in contact with their children but might live in a different part of the country. People are also living longer—often for 20 years after they've retired from their job. Modern American culture tends to value youth rather than age. All of this creates an interesting challenge for older people—and for the country, since by the year 2020, 1 in every 6 Americans will be over the age of 65.

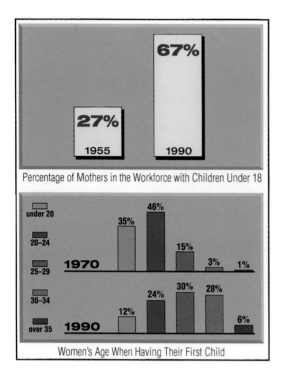

Percentage of Mothers in the Workforce with Children Under 18

67%
1990

27%
1955

under 20			
20–24			
25–29	**1970**		
30–34			
over 35	**1990**		

35% | 46% | 15% | 3% | 1%
12% | 24% | 30% | 28% | 6%

Women's Age When Having Their First Child

Future of the Family

Is the American family in trouble? People point to the divorce rate, to the fact that working mothers might have less time with their children, and to the "generation gap," or the problems that parents and children sometimes have understanding each other. Experts say, however, that the family is as strong as ever. Family is still at the center of most people's lives.

Discussion Points

- The passage describes several ways in which the American family is changing. Are families in your country changing? If so, are the changes similar to the changes in the United States?
- What do you think the perfect family is like? For example, how many children should there be? Should both parents work? Should the grandparents live with the family?

The Educational System

Education is for everyone.

Elementary School Through High School

There are three basic levels in the U.S. educational system—elementary school, which usually goes from kindergarten to sixth grade; junior high school, from seventh through eighth or ninth grade; and high school, from ninth or tenth through twelfth grade. Chil-

dren are required to be in school from the ages of 7 though 16.

About 90 percent of all children attend public school, which is free. The remaining 10 percent go to private schools, which often are associated with a religion. About half of all private schools are Catholic.

In the United States, education is mainly the responsibility of state and local governments, rather than the national government. The amount of money spent on education varies considerably from state to state. The subjects studied also vary somewhat. The school year usually runs from September to June.

At the high school level there are some specialized schools, including schools that emphasize vocational subjects like business or auto mechanics. Most high schools, however, are general schools. High school students are often involved in non-academic activities that their school offers—for example, in drama clubs, sports teams, or the school newspaper.

Advanced Schooling

Many students, upon finishing high school, choose to continue their education. Community colleges, also known as junior colleges, offer two-year programs. They are public schools and the tuition costs are usually low. Colleges and universities have four-year programs leading to a bachelor's degree (as well as, in many cases, further programs leading to higher degrees). These schools may be public or private; private schools cost a lot more. U.S. colleges and universities have many students from around the world, especially from Asia.

Trends in Education

Many more Americans than ever before are finishing high school and college. More than 20 percent of all adults have finished college, and more than 75 percent have finished high school.

Although the number of years of schooling is going up, there are signs that the quality of education may be going down. This is of great concern, especially since education is considered crucial to the American ideal that each person should achieve all that he or she can.

There are many theories about where the problems lie. Some think that students have too many "electives," or courses they choose, and too few courses in basic subjects. Others think students watch too much TV and do too little homework. Everyone agrees the problems must be addressed.

Write

What are some differences between the educational system in the United States and the educational system in your country? Read the passage again and then write a paragraph describing some of the main differences.

Culture, Leisure, Entertainment, Sports

The United States is an international center of culture. Its major cities (like New York, Boston, Washington, Chicago, San Francisco, and Los Angeles) regularly host many concerts, art exhibitions, lectures, and theatrical performances. And on a smaller scale, the same is true of smaller cities. Some of the world's greatest museums, orchestras, theaters, and concert halls are located in the United States. Performances and exhibitions are usually very well attended. Tickets can be hard to get, despite their high prices! Many cities also have large communities of artists, actors, dancers, and musicians.

The national and state governments, as well as private organizations, have traditionally supported the arts with money. Recently,

The New York Philharmonic

Americans love watching TV...

...and playing baseball in the park.

however, problems in the U.S. economy have decreased this support.

Though art and "high" culture are important in America, the most popular sources of entertainment and information are television, movies, radio, and recorded music. With cable TV, a lot more programs are available, but many people still complain about the low intellectual level of TV. They also feel that the emphasis on youth, sex, and money teaches children (and adults) the wrong values and goals. These criticisms are often made about American movies too. But despite the "bad" movies, many wonderful and internationally successful movies are produced in the U.S. The rapid spread of videotaped movies, watched nightly by millions of Americans in their homes, has made movies an even more popular and influential form of entertainment in recent years.

Most Americans enjoy sports—both playing sports themselves and watching their favorite sports and teams. Major professional sports events—baseball, football, basketball, and hockey, as well as golf and tennis—are witnessed by tens of thousands of fans, and by millions more on TV. Boys and girls play on sports teams in school and after school.

Many adult Americans regularly engage in sports like tennis, softball, golf, and bowling.

Americans also love to travel. Weekend automobile trips are a tradition for many families, as are longer summer vacation trips. Car travel is the most common leisure activity in America.

When Americans take car trips, they don't usually just drive and sightsee. They like to have a destination. Amusement parks, beaches, and other special attractions are always crowded when the weather is good.

Airplane travel is also common in America. At holiday time, many people fly to other cities to visit friends and relatives. During the winter, many people take short vacations to places with warm climates, like Florida and the islands of the Caribbean.

Discussion Points
- What are some popular leisure and entertainment activities in your country? What are some favorite sports? What are some favorite places to travel to?
- How about you? What do you like to do in your leisure time?

Holidays

Many people spend *New Year's Day* resting. That's because they've stayed up most of the night, greeting the new year! Some went to parties at friends' homes or at nightclubs. Others were out on the streets, throwing confetti and blowing noisemakers. Many people make New Year's resolutions (to eat less, to work more, etc.). Few people keep their resolutions.

In the 1950s and 1960s, Martin Luther King, Jr., led the civil rights movement—the struggle for equal rights for black Americans (see pages 66–70). King was assassinated in 1968. *Martin Luther King, Jr. Day,* which falls in January, around King's birthday, is a time to celebrate the life and achievements of this great American.

Two other great Americans are honored on *Presidents' Day.* George Washington was the country's first president. Abraham Lincoln brought the country through the Civil War (see pages 56–57 and 66–68). Their birthdays were both in February and are celebrated together.

Memorial Day honors American soldiers killed in war. There are many parades on Memorial Day. Memorial Day, which comes on the last Monday in May, is also the unofficial beginning of the summer vacation season. On Memorial Day, many people go to the beach.

The most important American holiday is the *Fourth of July,* or Independence Day. On July 4, 1776, the American colonies declared their independence from Britain (see page 52). Many families celebrate the Fourth of July by having picnics and, at night, watching fireworks.

Trick-or-Treating

Fourth of July fireworks

Labor Day honors the American worker. Just as Memorial Day means the beginning of summer, Labor Day, which falls on the first Monday in September, marks the end of summer. For many students, the school year starts the day after Labor Day.

Columbus Day celebrates Christopher Columbus's arrival in the Americas in 1492. As Columbus was Italian, working for Spain, Columbus Day is an especially important holiday for many Italian-Americans and Hispanic-Americans.

Although *Halloween,* on October 31, is not an official holiday, it is a very special day. On Halloween, children dress in costume as all kinds of things—as witches, ghosts, monsters, pirates, TV characters, and even computers and cereal boxes. The windows of many houses have Halloween decorations and jack-o'-lanterns. (Jack-o'-lanterns are pumpkins that have been carved with strange faces and have a candle inside.) In the evening, the children go from house to house, knocking on doors and saying "trick or treat." The people in the houses give the children candy or some other treat. If they don't, the children might play a small trick on them!

Thanksgiving dinner

Christmas morning

In 1620 one of the first British settlements in America was established in Massachusetts. These settlers, known as Pilgrims, had come to America to freely practice their religion. They arrived in November, when it was too late to plant crops. Although many people died, the Pilgrim settlement survived the winter because of help from Indians who lived nearby. The Indians taught the Pilgrims about corn and showed them where to fish. The next November, after the crops were harvested, the Pilgrims gave thanks to God at a feast to which they invited the Indians.

Every year, Americans celebrate *Thanksgiving.* Families and friends get together for a big feast. The meal usually includes roast turkey with stuffing and gravy, a sweet sauce made from cranberries, sweet potatoes, and pumpkin pie. What a meal! It's not surprising that a recent Thanksgiving tradition is to sit after dinner in front of the TV watching a professional football game.

Christmas, marking the birth of Christ in the Christian religion, is another time when many families get together. Christmas is an important time for giving gifts. In fact, people start buying gifts right after Thanksgiving, although Christmas is a month away. Many families put up a Christmas tree and bake lots of special Christmas cookies.

Small children believe that their gifts come from Santa Claus. Their parents tell them that Santa lives in the North Pole and, on the night before Christmas, he travels the world in a sled pulled by reindeer. He goes down the chimneys of houses to leave gifts for children who have been good. Naturally, children are the first to get out of bed on Christmas morning!

Quiz

What do you remember about the United States? Answer the following questions.

1. Where did the first people to settle North America come from?
2. In the years 1870–1930, what part of the world did many immigrants to the United States come from?
3. What two parts of the world are most immigrants from today?
4. Why does the U.S. Government have a system of checks and balances?
5. What are the two major political parties in the United States?
6. What written document set up the basic government of the United States?
7. Why does the United States have to import many resources?
8. What are some U.S. exports?
9. Does the United States have an official religion?
10. What is the single largest religious group in the United States?
11. What is a "reconstituted family"?
12. What is the "generation gap"?
13. How many basic levels are there in the U.S. educational system?
14. Do most American children attend public school or private school?
15. What does the Fourth of July celebrate?
16. On what day will you see many jack-o'-lanterns?
17. What was the reason for the first Thanksgiving?

Glossary

academic having to do with studies

achievement something good and important that a person has done

aging getting old

agriculture farming; **agricultural** characterized by farming

assassinate to kill someone, especially a politically important person

campaign *(v)* to try to get elected (by using ads, making speeches, etc.)

candidate someone who is trying to be elected to a political position

career a job, a profession

challenge *(n)* an interesting and important problem to be solved

commercial *(n)* an ad on TV

commonwealth a political unit that governs itself but is associated with a more powerful country

conservative a political view characterized by wanting things to remain the same

consist of to be made up of

consumer someone who buys or uses things

county the largest division of government within a state

culture the arts and way of life for a group or nation

decade a ten-year period (e.g., 1990–1999)

decrease to become less

degree an academic title given by a college or university to someone who has finished a course of study

discriminate against to treat members of a certain group in an unfair way

distinctive different

diversity the condition of having many different parts, of not being all the same

divorce *(n)* the legal end to a marriage

emigrate to move away from one's own country

establish to set up

executive having to do with carrying out laws

expert someone with special knowledge in a certain area

export *(v)* to send to a foreign country

feast a large meal with many good things to eat

festival a celebration, often with special events like music and dancing

foundation the base or starting point of something

harvest to cut and gather crops

immigrate to move to a new country to live; **immigrant** someone who moves to another country to live

import *(v)* to bring in from a foreign country

industrialization the process of developing an economy based on factories and the goods they produce

intellectual having to do with intelligence and with thinking

interference becoming involved in the business of others

interpret to make the meaning of something clear

judicial having to do with courts and with making judgments

lecture *(n)* a talk given to an audience

legislative having to do with making laws

leisure time free from work; activities done in free time

levels grades or stages of something

liberal a political view characterized by wanting to change things

literally exactly

majority more than half; most

migrate to move from one place to another; **migration** a movement of a group of people from one place to another

minority group a group that makes up less than half of the population (in the United States, often used for any group of Americans other than white Americans)

natural resources materials that come from nature and are used by people (minerals, fuels, etc.)

opportunity a chance

picnic a meal eaten outdoors, often as part of a trip

population all the people living in a place, country, or area

poverty the condition of being poor

prejudice disliking or having a bad opinion of people without reason

preserve to keep

principles basic ideas and rules

pumpkin a large, round, orange vegetable

region an area of a country

regulate to make rules for and have some control over

relative any family member

representative a person elected to serve in government; often used specifically for a member of the U.S. House of Representatives, the lower house of Congress

role task, function

salary money earned for work done based on a total amount for a year

shift a movement or change

sightsee to go and visit interesting places

single-parent family a family where there is one parent

slave a person owned by another person

society a community of people and its way of living

stimulate to help cause, to increase

succeed to do well, to have success

teenager someone aged 13 through 19

theory an idea trying to explain something

thoroughly completely; very

tradition something that has been done a certain way for a long time

train *(v)* to teach

transform to change greatly

treat *(n)* something that is good and special, particularly a sweet food

tuition money paid in order to go to school

unemployment the condition of not having work

values standards

vary to differ

wage-earner someone who works for pay

worship to take part in a religious activity

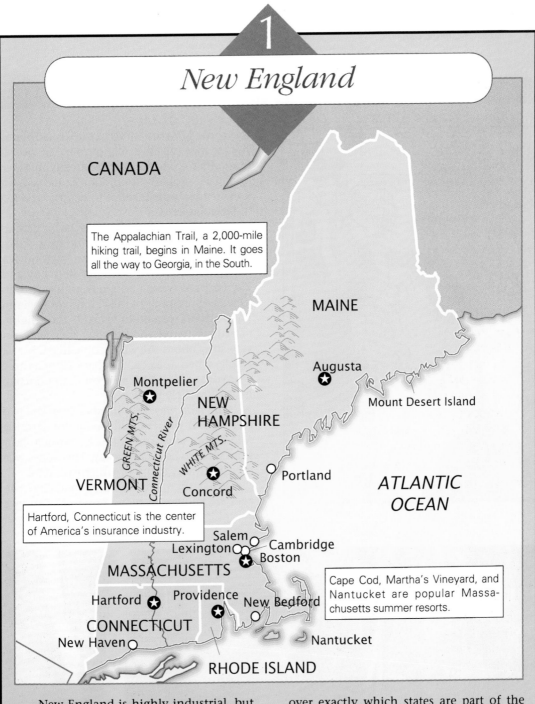

1

New England

CANADA

The Appalachian Trail, a 2,000-mile hiking trail, begins in Maine. It goes all the way to Georgia, in the South.

MAINE

Augusta ⭐

Mount Desert Island

Montpelier ⭐

NEW HAMPSHIRE

GREEN MTS.

Connecticut River

WHITE MTS.

Portland ○

ATLANTIC OCEAN

VERMONT

Concord ⭐

Hartford, Connecticut is the center of America's insurance industry.

Salem ○

Lexington ○ Cambridge ○

Boston ⭐

MASSACHUSETTS

Cape Cod, Martha's Vineyard, and Nantucket are popular Massachusetts summer resorts.

Hartford ⭐ Providence ⭐ New Bedford ○

CONNECTICUT

New Haven ○   Nantucket

RHODE ISLAND

New England is highly industrial, but it also has many fields, woods, and small towns. New England is the part of the United States that is most like "old" England. It is also the most well-defined region of the United States: Americans might disagree over exactly which states are part of the South, but for everyone New England includes six states—Maine, New Hampshire, Vermont, Massachusetts, Rhode Island, and Connecticut.

The New England Yankee

To people from the South of the United States, *Yankee* may mean a Northerner. To people from other countries, *Yankee* means an American. But, properly used, *Yankee* has a more specific meaning: It refers to people who live in New England.

The New England Yankee has a distinct character, shaped in part by the history and geography of the region. New England was settled in the 1600s by Puritans from England. The Puritans were a religious group who objected to the rituals of the Church of England. The Puritans wanted to "purify" the religion, making it stricter and simpler. They were also very strict about the way people lived. For example, when a sea captain back from a three-year voyage kissed his wife on their doorstep, he was publicly punished.

The land was even harsher than the people. Its soil was thin and poor for farming. And before any land could be farmed, large stones had to be cleared away. The stones were used for walls, many of which still exist.

What, then, is the Yankee character? Yankees are known for being honest but shrewd;

A New England stone wall

realistic and to-the-point; practical rather than romantic; untalkative, thrifty, principled, and independent.

Many stories illustrate the realistic and untalkative Yankee nature. In one story, a tourist asks a Maine fisherman whether the fisherman has lived in the same village all his life. "Not yet," the fisherman replies. In another story, a tourist who has lost his way in Vermont stops a couple to ask for directions.

"I want to go to Bennington," he says. "We've no objections," one of the New Englanders replies.

Calvin Coolidge, the thirtieth President of the United States, was a Yankee. Once he and a friend took a ride from Boston to a town 30 miles inland. "It's cooler here," Coolidge said as they returned to Boston. These were the only words he spoke during the entire trip. (When Coolidge was president, Americans called him "Silent Cal.")

Yankee thrift is well expressed by a New England saying: Eat it up, wear it out, make it do, do without.

Frederick Tudor, a Bostonian, is an example of the business shrewdness of the Yankees. As a young man, Tudor heard someone say jokingly that, if ice were a crop, New England would be wealthy. Tudor remembered this joke and, years later, figured out how to break up ice and ship it south. Tudor became a very rich man.

The Yankee character may partly explain the special role that New England has played in United States history. In the eighteenth century, the American Revolution began in New England. Yankees were among the strongest supporters of independence. In the nineteenth century, many New Englanders said slavery did not fit with their beliefs and principles. New England Yankees led the movement to end slavery in America.

"Ice Farming" in New England made Frederick Tudor a very rich man.

Words

The adjectives in the left-hand column were used in the passage to describe Yankees. Match each adjective with the best phrase from the right-hand column. People who are:

1. independent
2. honest
3. shrewd
4. realistic
5. untalkative
6. thrifty
7. principled

a. do not talk a lot
b. don't cheat other people
c. have strong ideas about what is right and what is wrong
d. use money and other things carefully
e. see things as they really are
f. don't let other people cheat them
g. do things themselves instead of asking others for help

A Yankee Replies

The passage gives two stories involving "typical Yankee" replies. Here is another story. What might the New Englander say?

A tourist in a New England town drives down Elm Street looking for a gas station. The tourist stops a man from the town. There is a gas station at Elm and Main Street.

Tourist: Excuse me, sir. Do you know where there's a gas station?
New England Yankee: _____

(For a possible answer, see page 171.)

Two New England Writers

A Witch's Curse

In the 1800s, when Nathaniel Hawthorne wrote his novels, the town of Salem, Massachusetts was a beautiful and prosperous seaport. But the novels look back to the 1600s, a dark period in Salem's history. The Puritans who ruled had very strict ideas and severely punished people who did not conform. In 1692, hysterical accusations made by some girls led to the Salem witchcraft trials. Twenty people were hanged as witches and many more were imprisoned. Finally, the governor of Massachusetts ended the trials when his own wife was accused of being a witch.

The Hawthorne family history was closely tied to Salem's. The first Hawthorne to settle in Salem was a judge. He once had five women tied to a cart and dragged through town; their "crime" was that they weren't Puritans. This man's son was a judge during the witchcraft trials. A woman he condemned to death put a curse on the Hawthorne family. There's no evidence that this curse had any effect on the Hawthornes. It did, however, show up in Nathaniel Hawthorne's writing.

The House of the Seven Gables tells of the Pyncheon family, who live under the curse of a man their ancestor condemned to death for witchcraft. The Pyncheons' lives are haunted by greed, violent death, false accusations, and slow decay—until one day love destroys the curse.

The House of the Seven Gables

Visitors to Salem can tour Hawthorne's home and also the House of the Seven Gables. This strange house belonged to Hawthorne's cousin. Today, tour guides will point out rooms and objects associated with Hawthorne as well as with his characters!

An Isolated Pond

Concord, Massachusetts was home to many American writers of the 1800s, including Hawthorne for a few years. Today their houses are open to the public. But perhaps the best-known dwelling in Concord is marked only by some stones and a chain. It wasn't even a house, but just a cabin near a pond. From 1845 to 1847, Henry David Thoreau lived in this cabin. There he wrote his greatest book, *Walden*.

The cabin at Walden Pond was Thoreau's experiment in living alone close to nature. Thoreau wrote, "I went to the woods because I wished to live deliberately, to front only the essential facts of life, and see if I could not learn what it had to teach and not, when I came to die, discover that I had not lived."

Thoreau's ideas and concerns are very relevant to our own times. Concerned with the destruction of the forests, he wrote, "Thank God they can't cut down the clouds." He believed that citizens had the duty of civil disobedience, that is, of peacefully protesting government policies they considered wrong. Thoreau practiced what he preached. In protest against the Mexican War, he refused to pay his taxes and consequently went to jail.

Visitors today can appreciate the isolated beauty of Walden Pond—unless they go in the summer, when the pond is a very popular swimming hole!

Complete

Hawthorne's most famous novels are set in the town of _____. One of Hawthorne's ancestors was a _____ at the Salem _____ trials. A woman he found guilty put a _____ on the Hawthorne family. Nathaniel Hawthorne used this theme in his novel _____.

Thoreau is known for his book based on his experiences at _____ Pond, near the town of Concord, Massachusetts. Thoreau believed that citizens had the duty of _____. To express his disapproval of the Mexican War, he refused to pay his _____.

(For the answers, see page 171.)

Discussion Points

- Do you agree with Thoreau's idea that civil disobedience is a citizen's duty? Do you think people should protest against government policies they disagree with? How do you think they should protest?
- Reread Thoreau's statement about why he went to live alone at Walden Pond. Do you think Thoreau's goals were important? Do you think living alone in nature is a good way to achieve those goals?

Walden Pond

The Sea

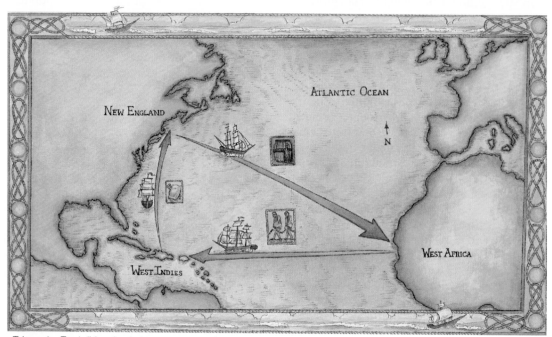

Triangular Trade" involved slaves, sugar, and rum.

From the time the first settlers discovered they could not expect much from the soil of New England, the sea played a major role in the region's economy.

In colonial times, New England prospered from fishing and trade. One kind of trade was the "triangular trade": New Englanders brought sugar up from the islands of the West Indies, used the sugar to make rum, took the rum to West Africa and traded it for slaves, and then sold the slaves in the West Indies.

Cod was the main fish export. Its importance was reflected everywhere—from graveyards, where an inscription reads:

Captain Thomas Coffin
Born Jan. 7, 1792. Died Jan. 10, 1842.
He has finished catching cod,
And gone to meet his God

to the Massachusetts Legislature, where the "Sacred Codfish" was prominently hung.

The American Revolution disrupted trade with England, and New Englanders had to find new trading partners. They soon were trading with Russia, Sweden, and even China. Whaling became an important activity. As the whaling industry grew, so did New England seaports like New Bedford, Salem, Marblehead, and Nantucket.

The mid-1800s were the era of the Yankee clipper ships. These elegant wooden ships, built in New England, were designed for speed and

Clipper ships in Boston Harbor

broke many records. When the 1849 Gold Rush (see page 155) suddenly populated San Francisco, clippers took goods to California. The trip around Cape Horn at the tip of South America was dangerous but worth it. The miners had gold and not much else. In California, goods were worth twenty times what they were worth in the East!

Since these trips were long and captains did not socialize with their crew, many captains took their wives along for company. The women from New England sea towns often knew as much about sailing as the men. When Captain Patten fell ill of brain fever while rounding Cape Horn in a storm, Mary Brown Patten, his 19-year-old wife, took command and sailed the ship safely to San Francisco.

The discovery in the 1850s of underground sources of oil marked the decline of the whaling era in New England. The days of the clipper ship ended even more quickly. The clippers simply could not compete with the metal steamships developed in England in the 1860s.

By the late 1800s, the sea no longer played such an important role in New England's economy. But money earned from the sea was used to build factories. The result was a new direction for New England's economy.

Word Search

Can you find ten words that are connected with New England shipping? All the words are from the passage. The words are written horizontally and vertically.

C	O	D	G	L	F	T	R	A	D	A
A	B	S	C	L	I	P	P	E	R	S
P	O	E	L	D	S	N	I	C	K	T
T	R	A	D	E	H	A	X	E	S	A
A	T	P	C	B	I	N	A	D	I	W
I	N	O	F	Z	N	T	P	Y	S	H
N	O	R	K	A	G	U	Q	R	H	A
I	L	T	I	S	H	C	L	P	I	L
S	A	L	E	M	A	K	N	E	P	I
T	N	S	A	N	T	E	C	I	L	N
S	E	L	T	B	G	T	E	M	P	G

(For the answers, see page 171.)

A Maine Vacation

A lighthouse on the rocky coast

A delicious clambake

A Maine vacation can be almost any kind of vacation you want.

A Maine vacation can be a seaside vacation along the state's rocky and winding coast. Glaciers and the sea have carved so many inlets and harbors that the 228-mile-long coast would be 3,478 miles if it were stretched out straight! Thousands of islands lie off the coast of Maine. Most are uninhabited and are visited only by fishermen. Many have strange names—for example, Wreck Island, the Hypocrites, Junk of Pork, Pope's Folly, and No Man's Land.

If you want to explore the coast and islands, you can hire a boat and a captain.

One large and well-known island is Mount Desert Island. Here you'll find the town of Bar Harbor, a very popular summer resort. If you get tired of the shops and crowds, you can visit Northeast Harbor, Southwest Harbor, and Somesville, the island's smaller towns. You can also go for a swim, although the water temperature is hardly ever over 55°F!

Maine is famous for its lobster. While you're near the sea, you might want to have some lobster or even a clambake—a traditional meal that New Englanders adopted from the Indians. Here's how you can prepare a clambake: First, pile up layers of logs and rocks. When burned, the logs will heat the rocks.

Cover the hot rocks with seaweed and then a rack. Put food on the rack in the following order: clams, potatoes and onions, chicken and fish, hot dogs, and—finally—lobsters and corn. Cover the food with a heavy cloth. In an hour you'll have a feast!

Maine's woods are perfect for a hiking and camping vacation. You might try Baxter State Park in the north. This 200,000-acre park is named after Percival Baxter, a governor of Maine who bought the land little by little and then gave it to the state. The park has many trails and campsites; some you can reach only by boat. (By the way, if you need any supplies,

Summer on a lake

Colorful autumn

Winter skiing

you can find them in Freeport, Maine at L.L. Bean, the outdoor clothing and equipment store. L.L. Bean is open 24 hours a day, every day of the year!)

Maine has hundreds of lakes and rivers for boating. Maine is also popular among hunters, because of its many deer, bears, squirrels, and rabbits.

In September, people drive through Maine to see the leaves turn all shades of red, yellow, and orange.

When the snows arrive—and they usually arrive early—skiers rush off to Maine's many mountains.

Depending on the kind of vacation you want, you can visit Maine at just about any time of year. The one time *not* to visit is May, when the fierce black flies make their yearly visit!

Discussion Point

Which of the following Maine vacations would you prefer to take?

(1) a seaside vacation
(2) a camping and hiking vacation
(3) a skiing vacation

Explain the reasons for your choice.

Find the Question for These Answers

Ask questions to get these answers.

1. It's hardly ever over 55°F.
2. Hot dogs are used, but not hamburgers.
3. Always; it never closes.
4. Don't plan it for May.
5. There are thousands.

Walking the Freedom Trail

The American Revolution lasted from 1775 to 1781. After March 1776, the city of Boston was never again touched by fighting. Yet no other city played as important a role in the struggle for independence. It was events in Boston that led to the revolution.

In the 1760s, England passed laws that imposed taxes on the colonists and limited their rights. Bostonians strongly objected. Riots in 1768 led to the occupation of Boston by British soldiers. From there, problems grew. In 1770, an angry crowd threw snowballs (evidently filled with stones and ice) at some soldiers. The soldiers then fired into the crowd, killing five men; this event became known as the Boston Massacre. In 1773, to protest a new tax, Bostonians, dressed as Indians, threw 400 crates of British tea into the Boston Harbor.

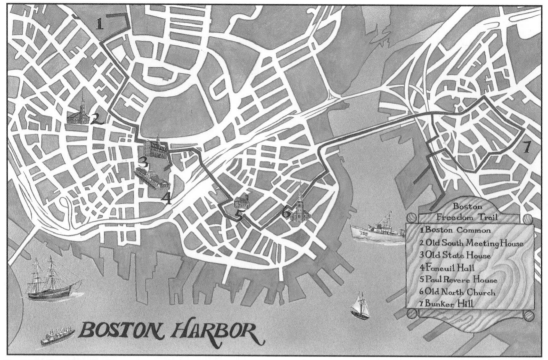

Boston's Freedom Trail

In response to the Boston Tea Party, Britain closed the harbor. This response was a severe one, since Boston depended on trade.

Before long, colonists in and around Boston began raising armies and preparing to fight if necessary. The first shots were fired in April 1775, in the nearby town of Lexington. Independence was formally declared, by Massachusetts and the 12 other colonies, on July 4, 1776.*

Visitors to Boston can see landmarks of the revolution by walking the Freedom Trail.

1. The Freedom Trail begins in the *Boston Common.* Today a public park, the Common was in the past a cow pasture, a public execution site, and a drilling field for soldiers. When the British occupied Boston in 1768, their troops camped on the Common. The British set off for Lexington and the first battle of the war, leaving the Common by boat. (To-day this wouldn't be possible; the area was long ago filled in to make more land!)

2. In times leading up to the Revolution, the *Old South Meeting House* was a church and, as its name suggests, an important meeting place for the people of Boston. Here leaders such as Samuel Adams and James Otis gave speeches that stirred up the colonists' emotions. Only hours before the Boston Tea Party, thousands met to discuss the tea tax. Later, British general "Gentleman Johnny" Burgoyne, as a deliberate insult, tore up the church benches and used the Meeting House to exercise horses.

3. The *Old State House* was the building from which the British had ruled Massachusetts. On July 18, 1776, the Declaration of Independence was read from its balcony. The statues of a lion and a unicorn, symbols of the British government, were then thrown down into the streets. The streets outside the State House were also the scene of the Boston Massacre, in 1970.

4. *Faneuil Hall,* sometimes called "the Cradle of Liberty," functioned as both a market (downstairs) and a meeting place (upstairs). The British took over Faneuil Hall and

---

*The thirteen American colonies were Massachusetts, New Hampshire, Rhode Island, Connecticut, New York, New Jersey, Pennsylvania, Delaware, Maryland, Virginia, North Carolina, South Carolina, and Georgia.

used it as a weapons storehouse and a theater. British officers were watching *The Blockade of Boston,* a comedy written by General Burgoyne himself, when someone cried out, "The rebels! The rebels! They're attacking Charlestown Neck!" The officers roared with laughter—until they realized the play had been interrupted by a scene from real life!

5. Paul Revere was a well-known silversmith and a hero of the revolution. The Freedom Trail continues to a neighborhood known as North Boston, where visitors can see *Paul Revere's House.* This house is the oldest in Boston. In the garden there is a large church bell made by Revere. Nearby there is a statue in honor of Revere's famous ride to Lexington.

6. The colonists knew the British planned to attack Lexington. But they did not know when or how the British would attack. Paul Revere said that when the British left Boston he would carry the word to Lexington. He asked another Bostonian to hang either one or two lanterns from the high steeple of *Old North Church.* One lantern would mean the British had left by land, two that they had left by sea. As he galloped to Lexington, Revere saw the two lights.

7. The last stop on the Freedom Trail is *Bunker Hill.* Colonists defended Bunker Hill against a much stronger British force. The colonists were defeated, but at a huge cost to the British. Bunker Hill convinced other colonists to fight. For the colonists, it was a victory in defeat.

True or False

_____ 1. Hundreds were killed in the Boston Massacre.

_____ 2. The Boston Tea Party was a meeting held to discuss a tea tax imposed by the British government.

_____ 3. The first battle of the Revolution was fought in 1775.

_____ 4. In the beginning, the Revolution took place mainly in Boston and the surrounding area.

_____ 5. Boston was occupied by the British throughout the Revolution.

(For the answers, see page 171.)

The Battle of Bunker Hill, by American painter, John Trumbull.

Cambridge

The ivy walls of Harvard University

Rowing on the Charles River

Just across the Charles River from Boston is Cambridge, America's most famous student town.

Cambridge is sometimes called the birthplace of American intellectual life: It has the nation's oldest university, Harvard University, founded in 1636. Cambridge remains a center of intellectual life, especially since it's also home to MIT, the Massachusetts Institute of Technology.

Harvard has an excellent reputation in many fields; MIT is a leader in science and technology. Students attending Harvard and MIT come from around the world; Harvard alone has students from 90 countries.

Since one-fourth of the people in Cambridge are students, it's not surprising that Cambridge has many bookstores, shops, restaurants, coffee houses, and clubs.

A common sight in Cambridge is Harvard oarsmen rowing on the Charles River. The Harvard rowing team spends all year preparing for races in the spring, especially for the Harvard-Yale Regatta. Yale University is Harvard's big rival.

Discussion Points

- Have you heard of Harvard University and MIT? If so, what else do you know about them? Would you want to go to either university? If so, which?
- Would you want to live in a town like Cambridge, with many students? Why or why not?

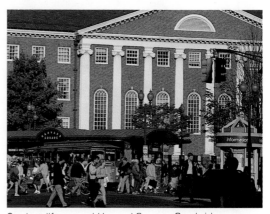

Student life around Harvard Square, Cambridge.

Boston Brahmins

John Singleton Copley painted Boston's elite.

Elites don't fit the American ideal of equality, and the United States has had few elites. The Boston Brahmins, however, were certainly an elite.

The Boston Brahmins were wealthy, well-educated, and exclusive. They were always Protestants and belonged to old Yankee families. Prominent among them were Cabots, Lowells, Peabodys, and Endicotts. These families often lived in Beacon Hill, an elegant part of Boston. They socialized in private clubs like the Somerset Club on Beacon Street. They married among themselves and gave their sons Brahmin names (Cabot Lowell, Lowell Cabot, Endicott Peabody). Their sons always went to Harvard.

The Boston Brahmins were very "proper"—they did things in established ways. Mrs. John Lowell Gardner, a wealthy New Yorker who married a Brahmin, shocked the community by posing for her portrait in a tight-fitting dress—not to mention taking walks with her pet lion!

The Brahmins were definitely exclusive. They did not like to socialize with other Yankees, and they especially looked down on the Irish Catholic immigrants who poured into Boston in the mid-1800s. In response, an Irish Bostonian wrote these now-famous sarcastic lines:

> And this is good old Boston,
> The home of the bean and the cod,*
> Where the Lowells talk only to the Cabots,
> and the Cabots talk only to God.

In our century, barriers broke down, partly because of the growing influence of a certain Irish-American family from Boston—namely, the Kennedy family. And yet, even after he was elected president, John F. Kennedy told a friend that he wasn't sure the Somerset Club would have him as a member!

---

*Beans baked for hours with dark sugar and bacon are a traditional dish in Boston, where winters are cold.

Sugaring Time

For a brief period each spring in Vermont it's sugaring time. When days are warm but nights are cool, sap begins to run in the sugar maple trees. The trees are then tapped and buckets are put under the taps, in order to collect the sap. The maple sap is boiled down in sugarhouses, until it becomes a thick, rich liquid known as maple syrup. Millions of trees must be tapped, since it takes four trees to get enough sap for a single gallon of syrup!

Collecting maple syrup from a tree

Maple syrup is good on vanilla ice cream. It is absolutely necessary on pancakes—the flat, flour cakes that Americans sometimes eat for breakfast. Some Americans may settle for imitation maple syrup, made in factories from water, sugar, and artificial colors and flavor. But the true pancake lover insists on having the real thing.

Puzzle

During sugaring time, the temperature changes each day from warm during the day to cool at night. See if you can change the temperature from "warm" to "cool." Do this by changing the starting word one letter at a time. You must form a word at each step. (In the example, there are only four steps between "warm" and "cool." Any number of steps is possible. Keep making changes until you get the word you want.)

Example: **warm**
worm
word
wood
wool
cool

Glossary

accusation a statement that someone has done something wrong

ancestor someone who was in your family long ago (great-grandmother, great-great-grandfather, etc.)

barrier something that stops you from passing

Brahmin a member of the highest social class (this word is borrowed from Hindu castes in India)

campsite a place where people camp

character your nature, what kind of person you are

clam a shellfish that is eaten as seafood

colony an area that is governed by another country

conform to go along with the rules, to behave in the expected ways

convince to make someone believe something

cradle a small bed for a baby; the starting point of an activity or movement

crate a large box usually made of wood

crop plants grown by farmers—fruits, vegetables, etc.

curse a strong wish for something bad to happen to someone

decay to become ruined, usually slowly over time

declare to say something firmly and clearly, especially in an official way

defeat (n) the losing of a game, fight, war, etc.

disrupt to bring or throw into disorder, to cause a change in something

distinct clear, easy to see, hear, or smell

dwelling a place where people live

elite a small group with a lot of money and/or power

emotion a mood or feeling

era a period of time

essential necessary

event something that happens

exclusive including only certain people and not including others

export (n) something one country sells to another country

feast a large and special meal

gallop to ride very fast on a horse

geography the land, climate, etc., of an area

glacier a huge piece of moving ice

hang to be killed by hanging from a rope around the neck, especially as capital punishment

harsh cruel, severe

hike a long walk, especially in the country

immigrant someone who comes from one country to live in another country

impose to force something on someone

industrial with many factories

inland away from the sea

inlet a bay or strait; a place where the coast goes in

landmark an important building or other important place, often easily recognized

lobster a shellfish with large claws

log a thick, rounded piece of wood from a tree

market a place where food and other things are sold

massacre killing of a group of people in a cruel way

miner someone who digs in the ground for metals or minerals like gold or coal

movement people coming together to reach a goal, especially a political goal

object *(v)* to disagree with, to not like

objection disagreements with something

policy general plan of a government, business, company, etc.

practice what you preach to behave in a way that fits with what you say

properly correctly

prosper to become wealthy, to do well financially

prosperous wealthy

relevant to have meaning for, to be important to

resort a place that many people visit on vacation

riot fighting in a crowd of people

role a part, a function; **play a role** to act a part (e.g., in a movie), to have a certain function

rum an alcoholic drink made from sugarcane

sarcastic using expressions that clearly mean the opposite to what is felt

seaport a town with a harbor used by large ships

seaweed a kind of plant that grows in the sea

settle to make your home in a new place

socialize to spend time with other people in a friendly way

struggle a big effort, a fight

trade *(n)* buying and selling

uninhabited not lived in

weapon an instrument for fighting

wear out to use something until it is completely finished

whaling hunting and killing whales for their oil

winding having many twists and turns

witch a woman who uses magic to do things

New York

Manhattan is an island just 13 miles long and 2 miles wide. It is the center of American finance, advertising, art, theater, publishing, fashion—and much more. The borough of Manhattan is what most people think of when they think of New York, one of the most exciting cities in the world.

New York attracts people from all over. Get on a subway in New York and look at the newspapers that people around you are reading. One person is reading a newspaper in Spanish, another in Chinese, yet others in Arabic, Russian, Italian, Yiddish, and French. New York was always a city of immigrants. It still is.

New York's other boroughs are Brooklyn, Queens, the Bronx, and Staten Island. Brooklyn alone has so many people that if it were a separate city, it would be the fourth largest in the United States!

Manhattan Geography

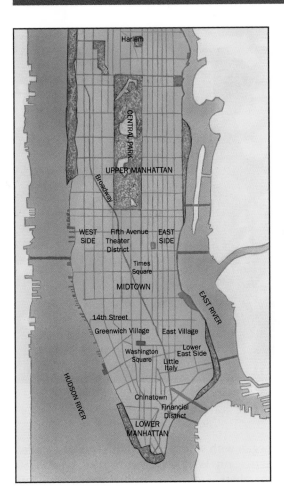

gins at Fifth Avenue, as does West 47th Street. (Avenues with lower numbers are on the East Side, avenues with higher numbers on the West Side.)

Manhattan is also divided, with less exactness, into Lower (Downtown), Midtown, and Upper (Uptown) Manhattan. As you go north, or uptown, the street numbers get higher. Lower Manhattan generally refers to streets below 14th Street, Midtown to the area between 14th Street and Central Park, and Upper Manhattan to the remaining, northern, part of the island.

Answer

Use the map and the passage to answer these questions.

1. The West Side of New York is bordered by the _____, whereas the East Side is bordered by the _____.
2. What are some areas in Lower Manhattan?
3. What divides the Upper East Side from the Upper West Side?
4. You want to go from 14th Street to 42nd Street. Do you take a bus that's headed (a) downtown, (b) uptown, or (c) crosstown (east to west)?
5. After seeing a Broadway play, you want to have a Chinese meal in an authentic setting. Will you go uptown or downtown?

It's said that in today's world to get where you're going, you have to know how to get there. This is certainly true in Manhattan! Many taxi drivers are recent immigrants, who don't fully know their way around. The subway system confuses even some longtime New Yorkers. And, when you want to ask for directions, people look like they're in too much of a hurry to stop and answer you.*

Manhattan is divided into the East Side and the West Side. The dividing line is Fifth Avenue. So, for example, East 47th Street be-

---

*Don't hesitate to ask for directions, though. People *will* stop. Contrary to the reputation they sometimes have, New Yorkers are generally friendly and helpful!

The Financial District

The main trading floor of the New York Stock Exchange

The Dutch were the first Europeans to settle Manhattan. To protect themselves from attacks, they built a sturdy wooden wall. Although it's now long gone, this wall gave its name to a street in Lower Manhattan and the street, in turn, became synonymous with American capitalism. The street, of course, is Wall Street.

It's easy to see why "Wall Street" means capitalism. The New York Stock Exchange and the American Stock Exchange are both in the Wall Street area. So are many stockbrokers, investment banks and other banks, and headquarters of many large corporations. There is also the Federal Reserve Bank of New York, a branch of the national bank of the United States—and the only branch that buys and sells government securities.

On any weekday you can visit the New York Stock Exchange. The Exchange, which began with several merchants meeting under a tree on Wall Street, now has over 1,350 members. From the visitors' gallery you can watch as trading goes on at a frantic pace below you.

Outside on the street, the pace is just as frantic (but only during working hours—the city's nightlife is elsewhere). The area's narrow streets and tall buildings can feel confining and can make the crowds seem overwhelming.

To escape the commotion of Wall Street, you can visit the nearby South Street Seaport. The seaport is an open area of low buildings on the East River. Long ago, this area used to be *in* the East River. Manhattan has always needed more space. Although space has mostly been increased by building up through skyscrapers, it has also been increased by making the island larger through landfills.

In addition to many shops and restaurants, the seaport has a museum. You can tour old houses, ships, and shipyards—reminders of the days when New York was above all a port. At the seaport, you can also tour the Fulton Fish Market, where city restaurants buy their fish—if you can be there at five in the morning!

Two good ways to get the larger picture of New York are to circle it in a boat and to hover over it in a helicopter. In the financial district, though, there's another way to see New York. The twin towers of the World Trade Center rise 1,350 feet above the city. There's an observation deck on the 107th floor of one of the towers. (Note: In the winter, the plaza between the buildings is closed, since an icicle falling from that height could kill!)

Appropriately, the very first business deal in Manhattan was made in what became the financial district. As every American schoolchild knows, the Dutch bought Manhattan from the Indians, for the ridiculously low price of 24 dollars worth of beads and trinkets. There is, however, another, less known side to this

Narrow streets in the Financial District

The South Street Seaport

The World Trade Center

story: Evidently, the Indians who had sold Manhattan did not themselves live there or in any sense own it! The Dutch and the Indians alike walked away pleased.

Discussion Points

- Do the large cities in your country have room to expand? Discuss how they have grown to fit more people. Are there any bad consequences?
- Because many of New York's older buildings were torn down to make room for taller buildings, some people feel that the city has lost much of its history. New York now has a landmarks commission, which decides whether changes can be made to buildings that are of historical interest. What has happened in the cities of your country? Do older buildings remain? Do you think government should be able to limit construction, the way that the New York landmarks commission does?

Puzzle

Use the clues to solve the crossword puzzle.
(For the answers, see page 171.)

Across

1. _____ Center
4. Buildings in the financial district are not _____
5. Abbreviation for the New York Stock Exchange
7. _____ Street Seaport
9. Sellers of Manhattan
10. A way to go around New York City
12. Original meeting place for the New York Stock Exchange
13. Sold at the Fulton Market

Down

1. Location of the New York Stock Exchange
2. Purchasers of Manhattan
3. River the South Street Seaport is located on
6. A way to go around New York City
8. Used to Purchase Manhattan
11. _____ Towers

The Lower East Side

The Lower East Side was originally an elegant neighborhood. When New York was the capital of the United States, President George Washington lived on the Lower East Side.

By the mid-1800s the Lower East Side had changed greatly. One of its buildings from this period was called Old Brewery. Old Brewery had two wings, nicknamed Murderers' Al-

Tenement life in the late 1800s

ley and the Den of Thieves. Police estimate that for many years there was an average of one murder per night in this building alone!

But the Lower East Side was characterized less by crime than by the poverty and hopes of its residents. By the mid-1800s the Lower East Side had become an area in which immigrants settled. First there were many Irish, then came many Jews from Eastern Europe.

The immigrants lived in crowded tenements. The population density of the Lower East Side in the 1880s was greater than that of Bombay, India. Working conditions were as bad as living conditions. Immigrants worked in "sweatshops" for long hours. After working six or seven days a week, they brought home as little as four dollars.

Life on the Lower East Side also had its pleasures, though, especially food. The egg cream was a mysterious New York invention—a drink containing not eggs and cream, but sparkling water and chocolate syrup. The candy stores of the Lower East Side made the best egg creams in New York. Other special foods included fish like herring, sour pickles, and "knishes," which are pastries stuffed with mashed potatoes or other fillings. All can still be found on the Lower East Side.

In recent years, many Jews have moved elsewhere, and the Lower East Side has become home to a newer immigrant group—Puerto Ricans and other Hispanics.

Near the Lower East Side there are two other neighborhoods that also attracted immigrants—and that are also famous for their food.

Italians settled Little Italy at the same time that Jews settled the Lower East Side. Like the Jews, many Italians have now moved to other neighborhoods. Little Italy has become littler. (It has also become less authentically Italian: although Martin Scorcese's movie *Mean Streets* was set in Little Italy, he decided to film it in the Bronx.) The Italian restaurants and cafés remain popular to tourists and Italians alike.

As Little Italy has grown smaller, its streets have become part of the neighborhood next door—Chinatown. For years, there were laws limiting the number of Chinese immigrants. Finally, the laws were changed. Today Chinatown is the only immigrant community in Manhattan that's still growing.* Chinatown has seven newspapers of its own. It also has nearly 200 restaurants.

Chinatown today

---

*Most of New York's recent immigrants settle in other boroughs, especially Brooklyn and Queens.

Complete the Comparatives

Make comparative sentences from the strings of words. The sentences should be grammatically and factually correct.

Example: The population density of the Lower East Side was the population density of Bombay, India. *The population density of the Lower East Side was greater than the population density of Bombay, India.*

1. In the 1700s, the Lower East Side was/elegant/in the 1800s and 1900s.
2. At first there were/Irish/Jews on the Lower East Side.
3. Little Italy used to be/Chinatown.
4. Chinatown has/people/it used to have.
5. Little Italy is/authentic/it used to be.

Role Play

Divide into groups of three. Two of you should discuss and decide on where you will eat—at an Italian restaurant, a Chinese restaurant, or a Jewish delicatessen. The third person is the waiter or waitress at the restaurant and will explain any items on the menu you are unfamiliar with and then take your order.

Food Glossary: bagel—a circular bread with a hole in the center; **blintzes**—a light dough wrapped around a cheese or fruit filling; **borscht**—cold beet soup; **cannelloni**—pasta stuffed with meat or other filling and baked in a sauce; **cannolli**—a pastry with a hard outside and a creamy filling; **fettucini**—long, flat noodles; **lo mein**—mixed noodles; **lox**—smoked salmon; **ravioli**—pasta squares with a filling (usually cheese); **tortellini**—pasta rings with a filling; **wonton**—dumplings with a filling.

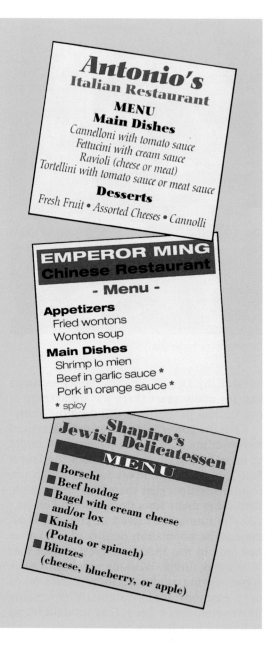

Antonio's
Italian Restaurant
MENU
Main Dishes
Cannelloni with tomato sauce
Fettucini with cream sauce
Ravioli (cheese or meat)
Tortellini with tomato sauce or meat sauce
Desserts
Fresh Fruit • Assorted Cheeses • Cannolli

EMPEROR MING
Chinese Restaurant
- Menu -
Appetizers
Fried wontons
Wonton soup
Main Dishes
Shrimp lo mien
Beef in garlic sauce *
Pork in orange sauce *
* spicy

Shapiro's
Jewish Delicatessen
MENU
■ Borscht
■ Beef hotdog
■ Bagel with cream cheese and/or lox
■ Knish (Potato or spinach)
■ Blintzes (cheese, blueberry, or apple)

Greenwich Village and the East Village

Greenwich Village and the East Village have always been at the center of New York's excitement. Both have been places for people with different and creative ideas. Both have an active nightlife with plenty of bars, restaurants, and clubs. But there are also clear differences between them.

Greenwich Village, more often called "the Village," is in many ways a residential area. It has homes on narrow, tree-lined streets.

Village Bohemians, 1920s

Tree-lined streets today

This charm attracted bohemians—writers and artists—to the Village in the early 1900s. The Village had other attractions, too:

> Nobody questions your morals,
> And nobody asks for the rent—
> There's no one to pry if we're tight, you and I,
> Or demand how our evenings are spent.*

The rents were cheap, and the artists, writers, and political radicals spent hours and hours in the cafés. Sex and revolution were openly discussed.

By the 1920s, the streets of the Village were filled with other people, curious to see how these odd Villagers lived. The artists and writers began moving out, some to the East Village.

Today, rents in the Village are far from cheap—they're much more than most artists can pay—but the tourists still visit. Some New Yorkers complain that the Village is "touristy" and "not authentic." But in fact the Village has many elements: students attending New York University; an active jazz scene; and in

Washington Square—its center—street performers, police, drug dealers, joggers, roller skaters, and just about everyone else. The gay (homosexual) community is an especially important part of Village life. The Village has many gay bars, and each year there's a Gay Pride march.

Washington Square Park

Tight here means "drunk." These lines are from a poem by Village resident John Reed, better known for his writings on the Russian Revolution.

An East Village "punk"

When bohemians moved to the East Village in the 1920s, they found an area similar to the Lower East Side: There were many immigrants, and although the buildings weren't tall, the area felt like a city. The dirt and grime of the East Village were a far cry from the quaint streets of Greenwich Village.

The East Village has changed very little. Immigrants, especially Ukrainians, live side by side with the area's younger residents. And the area still feels very city-like.

Over the years, the East Village has been a center for many movements—for the beat poets of the 1950s, the hippies of the 1960s, and, more recently, for New York's punk scene.

Scrambled Sentences
Unscramble the following sentences to learn more about Greenwich Village and the East Village.

1. the bohemians Italian arrived an Irish and neighborhood Before the Village was mainly
2. restaurants East Sixth Street Indian has both cheap and many are good that
3. rapidly The changes "club scene" very New York

(For the answers, see page 171.)

Midtown Manhattan

Office workers eat lunch outside in Midtown.

Many of New York's offices and jobs are in Midtown. So are many of its famous skyscrapers.

New York's first skyscraper was the Flatiron Building, built in 1902. Twenty stories high, it towered over the other buildings of its time.

The first building boom for skyscrapers came in the late 1920s. These skyscrapers were done in *art deco* style: They were highly dec-

The Chrysler Building

The Empire State Building

orated and elaborate. This was somewhat ironic, since when they opened, it was the Great Depression; the country's economy had collapsed.

The most beautiful and famous of the art deco skyscrapers are the Chrysler Building and the Empire State Building. You can't go to the top of the Chrysler Building, but you can admire it from many different points in the city. You can, however, go to the top of the Empire State Building, the third tallest building in the world. The Empire State Building has become not only a symbol of New York but also part of its history—both real, as when a plane crashed into it in 1945, and fictional, as when King Kong clung to it in the 1933 movie.

Rockefeller Center, built in the 1930s, is the world's largest privately owned business and entertainment center. Its nineteen buildings include the monumental RCA Building and Radio City Music Hall, where the famous Rockettes perform. Radio City is so luxurious and interesting that murals from its bathrooms now hang in the Museum of Modern Art.

Radio City Music Hall

The United Nations Building

The Seagram Building

In the 1950s, there was a second building boom, featuring a new style. The United Nations Secretariat building was the first *glass curtain wall* skyscraper. The Seagram Building, with its metal and its smoky glass, is another early example. The style became very popular; according to some people, Manhattan now has too many steel-and-glass skyscrapers.

When you are in Midtown, you can look at more than architecture. Fifth Avenue has stores that are among the world's most expensive—Cartier, Gucci, Tiffany's, and so on. They are great for window-shopping.

For more realistic prices, you can go to Midtown's department stores. Macy's, on the West Side, is the world's largest store, and Bloomingdale's, on the East Side, doesn't seem much smaller.

Answer
1. What style of architecture do the Chrysler Building and the Empire State Building represent?
2. What style do the United Nations Secretariat building and the Seagram Building represent?
3. Based on the pictures, describe the two styles. Then tell which you prefer and why.

The Theater District

Times Square
Perhaps nowhere are New York's extreme contrasts more obvious than in the Times Square area, around 42nd Street and Broadway. Beneath the bright neon signs of Times Square, you'll find some of New York's most elegant theaters and some of its sleaziest "adult" shows and shops.

The large numbers of police who patrol Times Square at night are there for a reason.

Times Square

When in Times Square, you should take basic precautions that are advisable anywhere in New York: Hold on to your pocketbook firmly, do not carry your wallet in your back pocket, and avoid wandering into areas with few people.

Times Square is named after the *New York Times,* which for years had its headquarters there. The *New York Times* is considered among the best newspapers in the country. New York's other main papers, the New York *Daily News,*

the *New York Post*, and *New York Newsday*, are tabloids—they have a smaller format and they focus, especially in their headlines, on crimes, scandals, and other such news. The *Village Voice*, a weekly newspaper with more liberal views than the other papers, has excellent listing of events around town.

On Broadway and Off

Times Square is the beginning of the theater district—the area where Broadway plays are performed. Most "Broadway" theaters are located east or west of Broadway on streets in the 40s and 50s. Broadway has long been the center of theater in the United States. Many plays open in other cities with the hope of eventually making it to Broadway.

In addition to Broadway there are Off-Broadway and Off-Off-Broadway theaters. Most of these theaters are in the Village and the East Village. (The category that a theater falls into actually depends on its size—with Off-Off being the smallest—not on its location.)

Plays at these other theaters tend to deal with a wider range of subjects and to be more experimental—some say more interesting—than plays on Broadway. They may involve audience participation—that is, the audience becomes part of the play. And at some Off-Off Broadway plays, you *feel* like you're part of the play because the theater is in someone's living room!

Interior of a Broadway theater before the crowds arrive.

A definite disadvantage of Broadway plays is the price of tickets. You can, however, get half-price tickets if you go to the TKTS booth in Times Square on the day of the play. Or perhaps you'd prefer to go backstage. There are tours of the stages of current Broadway plays, led by the stage managers, directors, and even famous actors!

Role Play

Divide into groups of three. Two of you should discuss which Broadway play you would like to see. Decide when you would like to go. Have a second choice in mind, just in case your first pick is sold out. When you have made these decisions, call the theater box office for tickets. The third person in the group is the ticket agent.

A Streetcar Named Desire – A Pulitzer Prize winning play about moral tensions in the South. Martin Buck Theater 555-0102 Mon.–Sat. at 8:00, Wed. and Sat. at 2:00 $37.50–$50 (2hrs.)

Oh Kay! – A fun musical with all your favorite Gershwin songs! Menskoff Theater 555-0374 Tues.–Sat. at 8:00, Wed. and Sat. at 2:00, Sun. at 3:00 – $40–$60 (2hrs. 20 mins.)

CATS – *The* famous Broadway musical that has warmed hearts around the world. The Spring Garden Theater 555-4895 Tues.–Sat. at 8:00, Wed. and Sat. at 2:00, Sun. at 2:00 $25–$60; 200 discounted tickets are available at the box office for students and senior citizens. (3hrs. 15 min.)

THE SOUND OF MUSIC – A romantic musical about the Von Trapp family and their unusual governess. Kentucky Theather 555-9370 Tues.–Sat. at 8:00, Wed. and Sat. at 2:00, Sun. at 3:00 $35–$55 (2hrs. 30 mins.)

Les Miserables – The long-running musical based on Victor Hugo's novel. In 19th century France, a cruel police inspector pursues a fugitive. (Tony Award winner) Empire Theater 555-1610 Tues.–Sat. at 8:00, Wed. and Sat. at 2:00, Sun. at 3:00 $30–$60; 150 discounted tickets are available at the box office for students and senior citizens. (3hrs.)

Central Park

The value of land in Manhattan has turned the island into a sea of concrete. Fortunately for New York's residents, there is one major exception: Central Park.

This huge park in the middle of the city was designed in the 1850s by landscape architect Frederick Law Olmsted. Olmsted wanted the park to be a rural paradise within an urban area, a place for all—"rich and poor, young and old." Central Park is still much as he intended.

You can take a horse and buggy ride through Central Park. You can explore the park even better by renting a bicycle. Attractions in the park include gardens, a zoo, a skating rink, an old-fashioned carousel, a lake where you can row, and an outdoor theater, where events are held each summer.

New Yorkers enjoy springtime in Central Park.

East Side

Central Park was opened in 1876. Wealthy New Yorkers soon built mansions along Fifth Avenue, on the park's east side. The Vanderbilts, a large family, at one point had eleven mansions on Fifth Avenue!

The mansions that remain now hold art collections. For example, there's the Frick Collection in what was once the home of millionaire Henry Clay Frick. The Frick is a delightful museum to wander through since it's set up, not like a museum, but as it was when the Fricks lived there.

This part of Fifth Avenue along Central Park has so many museums that it's called "Museum Mile." The Metropolitan Museum of Art, with huge collections of art from around the world, may be the most important museum in the United States.

The Metropolitan Museum of Art, cornerstone of "Museum Mile"

The Dakota

West Side

The street on the western side of the park, Central Park West, has large and unusual apartment buildings. When the first one was being built, people laughed. They said nobody with money would live in an apartment house, especially when it was so far from the center of town that it might as well be in the Dakotas (in the western part of the United States; see Unit 5). The builder had the last laugh; he named his building the Dakota, and when it opened, every apartment was occupied.

The Dakota has had many famous residents, including actress Lauren Bacall and conductor/composer Leonard Bernstein. But, above all, the building makes people think of John Lennon, who lived there and was killed right outside on December 8, 1980.

Harlem

Harlem Nightlife in the 1930s

In 1900, when the city extended the subway all the way uptown to Harlem, new housing was built there. For once, though, there wasn't a big need for housing in Manhattan, and the new buildings stayed empty. Then a black man approached the building owners with an idea: Why not rent to the black families, who wanted to move from the rundown housing they lived in downtown? It was in this way that Harlem became a largely black neighborhood.

The news soon spread that in Harlem blacks had better opportunities for housing and education. Many blacks came to Harlem from the south of the United States and even from the islands of the Caribbean.

The 1920s were Harlem's great years, especially in the arts. Top jazz musicians were heard regularly—Duke Ellington, Cab Calloway, Fletcher Henderson, Art Tatum, Fats Waller, and many others. Authors like Langston Hughes and Zora Neale Hurston began to write specifically about their experience as blacks.

Harlem had a very active club scene. Whites from downtown came to Harlem and partied until the early hours of the morning. Ironically, some of these clubs, including the famous Cotton Club, didn't allow blacks as customers. But people who lived in Harlem had parties of their own. At these parties, 50 cents bought lots of food and all-night piano playing. The music was probably better than anywhere else, as famous musicians came and "challenged" each other.

The depression of the 1930s hit Harlem hard. With a bad economy and ongoing discrimination, many blacks were unable to earn a living. The neighborhood became poorer,

The Apollo Theater today

and many middle-class blacks left. Harlem has never really recovered. Yet it has kept its special feel and remains a center for black culture. You can see this if you go on a tour of Harlem.

A tour might take you to churches where you can hear gospel music, to restaurants that serve soul food (food cooked in the way of blacks of the South), and to Harlem nightclubs to hear jazz. A club event you shouldn't miss is the Apollo Theater's Talent Night: Here, amateurs take their chances performing before an audience that is known for its enthusiastic applause and its equally enthusiastic boos!

Discussion Points

Read the article and discuss the questions.

NEW YORK — The city's crime rate has increased this year, official statistics show. The increase includes violent crimes.

Several recent murders involved innocent bystanders—people who just happened to be "in the way" when shots were fired.

Drugs and the ease with which sophisticated guns can be obtained appear to be factors contributing to the increase in violent crime.

The mayor's office has announced plans to hire and train more police officers.

When questioned by reporters, many New Yorkers said they would move elsewhere if they could. Other New Yorkers though, were steadfastly loyal to the city. They pointed out that the problems go beyond New York City. "For all its problems," one man said, "New York has so much to offer—concerts, plays, you name it. And besides, New York is my home."

- Has crime increased in the cities of your country? What do you think should be done to fight crime?
- Some New Yorkers want to stay in New York; others want to leave. What is your opinion? Would you want to live in New York? Why or why not?

Write and Talk

You have some friends who are stopping in New York for 24 hours on their way to San Francisco. Since you are more familiar with New York, they ask you what they should do there. Write a one-day itinerary for your friends.

Trade itineraries with a partner. Take turns roleplaying the person going to New York and the person giving advice. Discuss and explain the itinerary you have prepared.

Glossary

amateur someone who plays music, sports, for fun, not for money

authentic true, real, not fake

bohemian a person who does not follow the usual social rules of life

boom a rapid growth or increase (e.g., a building boom means many new buildings)

borough one of the five administrative units into which New York City is divided

corporation a business company

category a group, a type

club nightclub

contrary to opposite to, different from

depression period when the economy does poorly and many people are out of work

discrimination treating things or people in a different (often unfair) way

district neighborhood, area

elaborate *(adj)* fancy, with many details

element anything that is a basic part of something larger

estimate *(v)* to make a guess that should be close to accurate

experimental involving experiments or new ways of doing things

extend to spread out to

finance related to money and to managing money

frantic extremely fast, out of control

gospel music American religious music

headquarters main offices, especially of a company or group

housing *(n)* any buildings that are for people to live in

ironic expressing the opposite to make a point

landfill layers of soil, garbage, etc., built up to increase the amount of land and/or height of land

landscape architect someone who plans parks and other open areas for public use

mansion a large, fancy house

monumental big and impressive

mural art painted on a wall

nickname *(v)* to make up a descriptive name for someone or something

opportunity a good chance to get ahead

pace rate of speed

paradise heaven; a wonderful place

party *(n)* a festive gathering; *(v)* to participate in a festive gathering or celebration

period some amount of time

pickle a cucumber that has been preserved in vinegar

punk a loud, sometimes violent music style that emerged in the 1970s

radical *(n)* someone who wants major political and social changes

range an area

recover to get better again

regularly on a usual basis, often

resident someone who lives in a place (e.g., in a neighborhood, a city, a country)

residential mainly for living in, having many homes

rural related to the country and life in the country

sleazy cheap, dirty, crude

stockbroker someone who buys and sells securities (stocks and bonds)

sweatshop a factory or other workplace where conditions are bad and hours are long

synonymous having the same meaning

tenement an apartment building that is crowded and in bad condition

trinket small piece of jewelry; something that is not worth much

urban related to the city and city life

window-shopping looking in stores but not buying

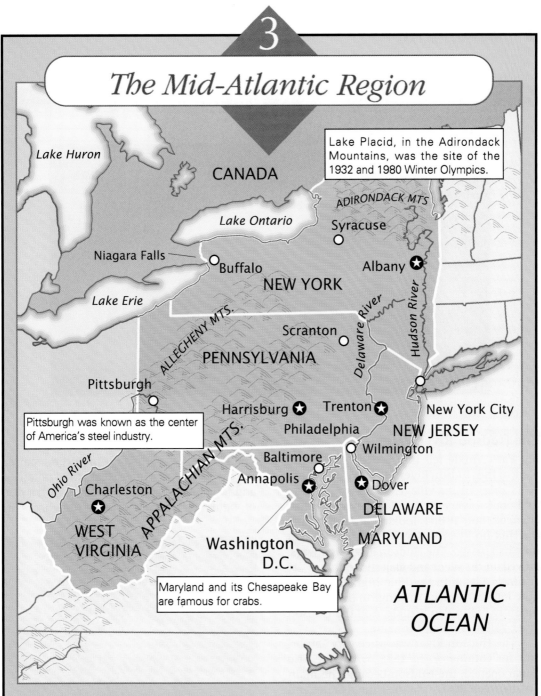

3

The Mid-Atlantic Region

Lake Huron

CANADA

Lake Placid, in the Adirondack Mountains, was the site of the 1932 and 1980 Winter Olympics.

ADIRONDACK MTS

Lake Ontario

Syracuse

Niagara Falls

Buffalo

Albany ★

NEW YORK

Lake Erie

Delaware River

Hudson River

ALLEGHENY MTS.

Scranton

PENNSYLVANIA

Pittsburgh

Harrisburg ★   Trenton ★   New York City

Pittsburgh was known as the center of America's steel industry.

Philadelphia   NEW JERSEY

APPALACHIAN MTS.

Wilmington

Ohio River

Baltimore

Annapolis ★   Dover ★

Charleston

DELAWARE

★

WEST VIRGINIA

MARYLAND

Washington D.C.

Maryland and its Chesapeake Bay are famous for crabs.

ATLANTIC OCEAN

The Mid-Atlantic region is by no means uniform: Geographically, historically, and economically, the Mid-Atlantic states are quite different from one another. New York borders on Canada and has cold winters; Maryland has much in common with the American South.

The Mid-Atlantic region plays an important role in the United States. Its cities include Washington, D.C., the nation's capital, and New York City, the nation's financial center. Not surprisingly, the Mid-Atlantic region is densely populated: Although the region is relatively small, nearly one in every ten Americans lives there.

New York Is Also A State!

The beauty of the Hudson River Valley inspired America's early painters.

The Hudson River Valley

Rip Van Winkle fell into a deep sleep on a bank of the Hudson River. He woke up twenty years later! In his village, as he would soon find out, everyone and everything had changed. But, at first, looking around him at the Hudson River Valley, he had no idea that time had passed. The Hudson River, as always, moved on "its silent and majestic course, . . . at last losing itself in the blue highlands." It is now 150 years since Washington Irving wrote the story of Rip Van Winkle. And the Hudson River Valley is much the same.

The Hudson River was once very important for commerce. In 1825, when the Erie Canal opened, the Hudson became the main link between the East of the United States and the growing Midwest. This made New York City, at the mouth of the Hudson, the nation's most important port.

But, even when it was commercially important, the Hudson River—with its fogs and mists, its green banks, and with mountaintops in the distance—was above all a romantic, mysterious, and beautiful river. Its beauty inspired not only writers like Irving, but also America's first group of painters, who became known as the Hudson River School.

Cooperstown

The Babe often partied all night and started the day by eating a huge steak, fried potatoes, and four fried eggs, washed down with a pint of bourbon whiskey. Then—somehow—he

Babe Ruth hits a home run.

would go out to the ballpark and hit home runs. He led the New York Yankees to victory year after year. In the days when baseball salaries were still small, his was large. When a reporter pointed out that he earned more than President Hoover, Babe Ruth replied simply, "I had a better year than he did."

The National Baseball Hall of Fame and Museum is located in Cooperstown, New York. There you can see exhibits connected with Babe Ruth and other famous players. Do you have great baseball potential? Probably not. But at the Hall of Fame you can test yourself by trying to hit balls thrown at the same high speeds as the balls that professional players hit.

Niagara Falls

Spectacular and beautiful, Niagara Falls has always been especially popular with two kinds of visitors: thrill-seekers and honeymooners.

It's easy to see why the thrill-seekers have visited Niagara. In 1859, Frenchman Jean Francois Gravelet, known as "the Great Blondin," became the first person to cross the falls on a tightrope. Not satisfied with this achievement, he made the trip again, this time with his manager on his back! In 1901, a schoolteacher, Mrs. Annie Edson Taylor, became the first person to go over the falls in a barrel.

It's less easy to see why so many newlyweds feel they have to begin married life at the falls. We do, however, know when and how this tradition got started: In 1803, Jerome Bonaparte, a nephew of Napoleon, visited Niagara Falls with his bride.

You don't, of course, have to be a newlywed to visit Niagara (and you *shouldn't* be a thrill-seeker, since stunts are now illegal). Each year many people visit from either the American side or the Canadian side. A boat called *Maid of the Mist* will take you right out to the falls!

Niagara Falls

Write

After sleeping for twenty years, Rip Van Winkle found his world had greatly changed. In our times, change is much more rapid. Imagine that you slept for twenty years. Write a paragraph describing what you might see and experience upon waking.

Discussion Points

- Today a baseball star might earn as much as 7 million dollars a year. In your opinion, are large salaries for professional athletes justified? Why or why not?
- Some people say that because athletes earn so much and because children admire them, athletes should be good role models—that is, set a good example by their behavior. Do you think athletes have this obligation?

Philadelphia, Pennsylvania

The Declaration and the Constitution

Philadelphia, Pennsylvania is the city where the two most important decisions in American history were made.

The Liberty Bell

In May 1775, representatives of the thirteen colonies met in Philadelphia to decide whether to remain with Britain or fight for independence. Fighting had already begun, but many people still hoped for peace with Britain. Finally, more than a year later, on July 4, 1776, the Declaration of Independence was unanimously approved. The Declaration says that independence is a basic human right:

> We hold these truths to be self-evident, that all men are created equal, that they are endowed by their Creator with certain unalienable Rights, that among these are Life, Liberty, and the pursuit of happiness. . . .

When independence was won, the colonies came together, not as a nation, but as a confederation, or group of states. To prevent tyranny, there was no president and the central government had very little power. Each state had its own army. The states taxed each other's goods. It was almost as if they were separate countries. The result was great confusion.

In 1787, representatives from all the states met in Philadelphia to discuss the

The Declaration of Independence, by John Trumbull

problems. They soon decided that the confederation could not work and that a new system of government was needed. For this purpose, they wrote the United States Constitution. The Constitution united the states into one country. For over two hundred years, it has provided the framework for American government.

Benjamin Franklin

One reason why the Declaration and the Constitution were written in Philadelphia is that in the late 1700s Philadelphia was America's most important city. Philadelphia's importance had much to do with one man—Benjamin Franklin.

In 1723, at the age of 17, Benjamin Franklin ran away to Philadelphia, looking for work as an apprentice printer. A few years later he had his own print shop and was publishing one of the most widely read newspapers in the colonies. Franklin did a lot for Philadelphia—for example, he started a library (the first in the colonies), a fire department, a city hospital, and a school that is now the University of Pennsylvania.

Franklin also did a lot for his country. He helped write the Declaration of Independence. During the war, he persuaded the French

to aid the colonists; without French help, the colonists might not have won the war. When the Constitution was being written, Franklin solved some serious disagreements; at 81, he was twice as old as most of the other men and was greatly respected.

Benjamin Franklin, by Joseph Siffred Duplessis
(© 1981 by the Metroplitan Museum of Art)

Benjamin Franklin was also a writer, philosopher, scientist, and inventor. In a famous experiment with a kite and a key, he proved that lightning is electricity.

20th-Century Philadelphia: A Boring City?

By the nineteenth century, Philadelphia lost its early importance. Washington, D.C., replaced it as the center of government. New York replaced it as the center of finance and trade.

Next to Franklin, the most famous Philadelphian may be comedian and actor W. C. Fields (1880–1946). W. C. Fields considered his hometown a truly boring place. "I spent a week in Philadelphia yesterday" was one of his well-known comic lines. Rumor has it—incorrectly, however—that his tombstone says "On the whole, I'd rather be in Philadelphia."

W.C. Fields

Is Philadelphia a historically important but otherwise boring city? Anyone who thinks so hasn't been there for the New Year's Day Mummers Parade!

Mummers are members of special string bands, and the parade is an all-day party. For the parade, mummers wear costumes covered with feathers and sequins. While they play and parade, they do a special dance called strutting.

Strutting is hard to resist. One spectator reports seeing an old woman break away from the crowd and start strutting alongside a band. As a police officer led her back to her place he, too, started strutting!

Mummers on parade

Complete

Use information from the passage to complete the rhyme.

In the beginning the states were not a _____.
They were merely a _____.
Representatives met in _____ to find a solution.
And there they wrote the _____.

(For the answers, see page 171.)

Sayings

Benjamin Franklin was known for his humor and common sense. When the Declaration of Independence was being signed, one man called for unity by saying, "We must be unanimous; we must all hang together." Franklin replied with a play on words: "Yes, we must indeed all hang together, or assuredly we shall all hang separately!"

Franklin's many sayings show his common sense. Here are some sayings that he made up. Can you tell what each means? Are there sayings with similar meanings in your language?

1. Remember that time is money.
2. Little strokes fell great oaks. (Here, *to fell* means "to cut down;" *strokes* is "swings of an axe.")
3. God helps them that help themselves.
4. Experience keeps a dear school but fools will learn in no other. (Here, *dear* means "expensive, costly.")

The Boardwalk

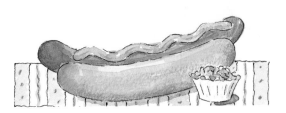

Now many beach towns in the United States have boardwalks. In many ways, all boardwalks are similar. Boardwalks usually have rides and games. They have shops that sell cheap souvenirs and junk food. They have benches that are perfect places to sit and watch the world go by.

But each boardwalk also has its own character and its own specialties. If you're in Atlantic City, be sure to get some saltwater taffy (a sticky, chewy candy). If you're on the boardwalk in Coney Island, in Brooklyn, New York, try a foot-long hot dog instead.

A train conductor on the line to Atlantic City, New Jersey, grew tired of the sand his passengers tracked onto the train. He thought of a solution. If a wooden walkway of boards was built above the sand, people could still enjoy the beach but his train would stay clean. And so the world's first boardwalk was built.

People liked the boardwalk so much that Atlantic City was soon transformed from a quiet resort into a booming one. As Atlantic City grew, so did the boardwalk. The first boardwalk was just 1½ feet above the sand and 10 feet wide. Today's boardwalk stands far above the sand and is 60 feet wide and 6 miles long.

Over the years, various other improvements were made. An early complaint, for example, was that "nearly every day somebody falls off the boardwalk. In nearly every instance, the individual has been flirting." Railings were the only practical solution to this problem!

Atlantic City honored its boardwalk by making it an official street. It is properly written as the Boardwalk, with a capital *B*.

A ride on the boardwalk

Puzzle

Why do people go to the beach and boardwalk? To find out, unscramble the words and read down. The clues will help you.

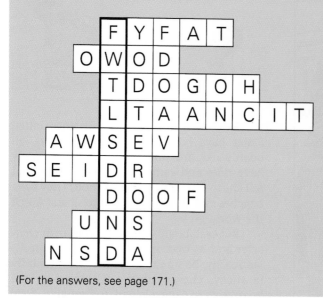

1. A sticky candy

2. Boardwalks are made of this

3. A Coney Island treat

4. Body of water many U.S. beaches are on

5. Surfers wouldn't go to a beach that didn't have them

6. A roller coaster is one

7. You'll never go hungry on the boardwalk, they always have this

8. You can't get a tan without it

9. The conductor didn't want it on his train

(For the answers, see page 171.)

The Nation's Capital

A view of Washington, D.C. in 1830 (detail)

Building a New City

With its grand neoclassical buildings and its tree-lined avenues, Washington, D.C. strikes the visitor as a lovely and formal city. Washington wasn't always this way.

When it was decided that the new country needed a new city for its capital, President George Washington himself helped pick the spot—a marshy area where the Potomac and Anacostia rivers come together. French engi-

Washington, D.C. today

neer Pierre Charles L'Enfant created a design based on Versailles, a palace built for King Louis XIV in the 17th century. The capital city would be crisscrossed by broad avenues, which would meet in spacious squares and circles.

Creating Versailles from a marsh was no easy task. Building went slowly, and people were reluctant to move to the new capital. For years, pigs roamed through unpaved streets. There was said to be good hunting right near the White House!

Matters were not helped when, during the War of 1812, the British burned parts of Washington. This episode did, however, give the White House its name. The president's house was one of the buildings burned, and after the war it was painted white to cover up the marks.

Museums and Monuments

People often save old things in the attic of their house. Nineteenth-century writer Mark Twain called the Smithsonian Institute "the nation's attic." This comment is even more true today, when, with its thirteen museums, the Smithsonian has at least a little of everything!

The Smithsonian began in the 1850s, with a gift from Englishman James Smithson. Although Smithson had never set foot in the United States, he left his entire fortune to this country, asking that it be used to found "an establishment for the increase and diffusion of knowledge."

Of all the Smithsonian museums, the most visited—indeed, one of the most visited museums in the world—is the National Air and

One of the buildings of the Smithsonian Institute

Capitol Hill

Space Museum. The museum has aircraft and spacecraft that were important in aviation history. It has the craft in which Orville Wright made the first manned flight and the plane in which Charles Lindbergh made the first solo flight across the Atlantic. It has the command module that returned the *Apollo 11* astronauts to earth after their moon landing, and it even has rocks that the astronauts brought back!

The Smithsonian buildings are built on or near the Mall, a large open space. The Mall also has monuments honoring George Washington and Abraham Lincoln. Washington was the first president. Lincoln was president during the Civil War and ended slavery. Many important civil rights events have taken place at the Lincoln Memorial. A third important president, Thomas Jefferson, who was also the main author of the Declaration of Independence, is honored by a monument overlooking the nearby Tidal Basin. The Tidal Basin area is especially beautiful in spring, when its many cherry trees, a gift from Japan, are in bloom.

Washington at Work

Washington has one major business, and that business is government. The executive departments (Treasury, Agriculture, Education, etc.; see the Introduction) are located in Washington. Many of the people who live in Washington work for the federal government.

When you're in Washington you can tour the White House, at 1600 Pennsylvania Avenue. You won't be able to see the president at work though; White House offices, as well as living quarters, are closed to the public. However, if you visit Capitol Hill, you might be able to see some important members of the other two branches of government: The Supreme Court has a public gallery, as do the Senate and the House of Representatives.

To go to the Senate or House gallery, stop in at any congressperson's office for a pass. Don't be surprised, though, if from the gallery you see a congressperson giving a speech to a nearly empty room! Absent members of congress are probably at committee meetings, where much of the important work is done. The public can also go to many of these meetings.

Congress and the public listen to a speech. (*Pamela Price/Picture Group*)

Write

Being a museum guard isn't easy—there are always so many questions to answer. A guard in the South Lobby of the National Air and Space Museum gives these answers to some frequently asked questions. Use the floor plan to figure out what questions the guard was asked.

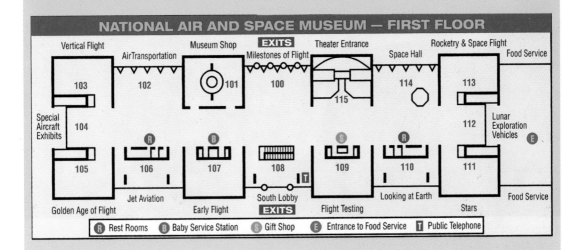

1. _____?
   "That exhibit is by the other exit, just across the hall."

2. _____?
   "When you walk out of the lobby, go right. It's all the way at the end of the hall with entrances to the left and the right."

3. _____?
   "There is one here in the lobby."

4. _____?
   "Make a left in the hall and it will be the first room on your right."

5. _____?
   "Of course, the museum has some, sir. Go left to 'Jet Aviation' or right to 'Looking at Earth.'"

Game

In five minutes' time how many words can you make from the word *Washington?* When the time is up, the person who has made the most words wins.

Here's another way to find the winner: The person with the longest list reads his or her words. When the person reads a word you wrote, draw a line through it. The person with the *most words that no one else has* is the winner.

Decide in advance which way you will play.

False to True

The following statements are all false. Rewrite the statements so that they will be true.

1. The city of Washington was designed by President George Washington himself.

2. The White House is named after the architect who designed it (Charles White).

3. James Smithson, whose money the Smithsonian Institution was started with, was an Englishman who had often visited the United States.

4. One of the Smithsonian museums—the Arts and Industries Building—is the most visited museum in the world.

5. The Mall has monuments honoring three important Supreme Court justices.

6. If the Senate chamber seems nearly empty, it's probably because most senators are out to lunch.

West Virginia: An Appalachian State

The Appalachian region is among the most rural—and beautiful—areas in the United States. It includes parts of thirteen states from New York to Georgia. West Virginia is the only state that falls entirely within the Appalachian region.

The Appalachian region is mountainous. The mountains have shaped people's way of life. Settlers, who came mainly from Great Britain and Germany, found themselves isolated by the mountains. According to an old joke, the only way to get to some mountain

The Hatfield clan of West Virginia

towns is to be born there! Isolation made it possible for people to develop and preserve their traditions.

The mountains also made earning a living difficult. Many Appalachian traditions center on handicrafts, as people had to make the items they needed. Appalachian people are known for their independence and their self-sufficiency. The motto of West Virginia is *Montani Semper Liberi* ("Mountaineers are always free").

Sometimes the ruggedness of mountain life was associated with violence. The Hatfield family lived in West Virginia; the McCoy family lived right across the border, in Kentucky. No one knows exactly what caused the trouble between the Hatfields and the McCoys. It may have been a pig that both claimed to own. In any event, the McCoys killed a Hatfield. The Hatfields took justice into their own hands, killing several McCoys. The Hatfield-McCoy feud lasted nearly forty years. It took many lives in both families.

Coal mining has long been an important activity in West Virginia; it contributes about 10 percent of the state's income. Mining brought some prosperity but at a cost. Before the establishment and enforcement of safety laws, many men died in mine collapses. Strip mining—in which land is blasted to get to coal close to the surface—destroyed some once-

Musicians playing mountain dulcimers

beautiful land. This was the fate of the town of Paradise, referred to in the following song:

> "And, Daddy, won't you take me back to Muhlenberg County,
> Down by the Green River where Paradise lay?"
> "Well, I'm sorry, my son, but you're too late in asking;
> Mr. Peabody's coal train has hauled it away."*

Handicrafts and Traditions

Quilting is a well-known Appalachian handicraft. A quilt is a bed cover, made of two layers of fabric stuffed with cotton. Using scraps of fabric, Appalachian women sewed squares, based on fancy patterns. They then sewed the squares together to make the two sides of the quilt.

To sew a quilt, a woman often called all her friends together for a big party known as a "quilting bee." When a quilt was finished, four girls would each grab a corner. A cat would be thrown onto the quilt, and the girls would shake the quilt up and down. The cat would, of course, run off the quilt. The girl it ran closest to would be the next to get married!

An Appalachian proverb says that "God respects you if you work, but he loves you if you sing." Several musical instruments, in-

Quilting

---

*Paradise was located in eastern Kentucky, near West Virginia; the Peabody Coal Company mined the area.

cluding the mountain dulcimer, were first made in the Appalachian region. Appalachian music is like American country music, but also like traditional English and Scottish ballads.

In a way, the Appalachian dialect is itself traditional. It is closer than any other dialect of American or British English to the English that was spoken in Shakespeare's time and earlier. For example, *n* is added to the end of pronouns (e.g., *hisn, hern, yourn*) and *a* is added to the beginning of verbs (*a-talking, a-coming*). Does the Appalachian term *bone-box* for "body" seem strange? You'll find the same word in *Beowulf,* the famous poem from eighth-century England!

Discussion Points
- Do you have any areas in your country that were geographically isolated? If so, did these areas develop strong traditions of their own?
- Appalachia is economically one of the poorer areas in the United States. When workers from the government visited the region to see what they could do, one older man told them, "Bring us your prosperity but leave us our civilization."

What did the man mean by this?
Do you agree with what he said?
Do you think what he wanted is possible?

Glossary

aid to help

alongside next to

apprentice a person who works for someone else to learn to do a particular kind of work

attic a storage space between the ceiling and the roof of a home

aviation flying in aircraft

ballad a song that tells a story, often a romantic story

ballpark a place where baseball is played

bank the land at the side of a river

baseball a game in which players on two teams hit a ball and move around bases

blast to blow up with explosives

boring dull, not interesting

civil rights the rights of citizens; the movement to gain equal political, social, and economic rights for black Americans

collapse to fall down, to fall in

comedian a person who makes people laugh

comic (adj) causing people to laugh

commerce trade, business

committee a group of people chosen by others to plan and organize

country music folk music of the U.S. South and West

dialect a language as it is spoken in a particular region

disagreement lack of agreement, differences of opinion

earn a living to work to pay for the things you need

enforcement causing to be obeyed, used especially for laws

episode an event; one event in a series of events

exhibit a group of objects shown in a museum

feud a long-lasting quarrel or fight between two families or groups

flirting playful teasing about love

formal following rules strictly, often used with dress, manners, or design

framework the basic structure supporting a system

grand great, impressive

handicrafts items made by hand, especially items that have a practical use but are also artistic

home run in the game of baseball, a hit that allows a player to score immediately

illegal against the law

inspire to encourage to do something, especially something creative

isolated separated from other people or places

link a connection between two things

marsh an area of low, wet land

matters the situation

mountainous having many mountains

motto a saying, especially one that expresses an important belief

mouth the place where a river opens into a larger body of water

neoclassical a style of art, based on the style of ancient Greece and Rome

on the whole when all things are considered

potential ability

proverb a popular saying, often about everyday life

relatively compared to others

reluctant not eager, not wanting to do something

representative someone who represents, or acts for, others, especially in politics

respected honored, thought well of

ruggedness roughness

rumor gossip, something that people say that might or might not be true

salary the amount of money earned for work, especially over the time of a year

self-evident obvious

self-sufficiency ability to take care of oneself without help from others

spacious having lots of space

spectacular amazing, very impressive

strike as to seem like

surface the outside or upper level of something

tombstone a memorial marker set up over a grave

tradition a custom, a way of doing things that has been used for many generations

tyranny a ruler's cruel or unjust use of power

unalienable (inalienable) not able to be taken away

unanimously with every person in agreement

uniform *(adj)* the same everywhere

4

The South

North Carolina is the center of America's tobacco industry.

Nashville, Tennessee is the center of country music and home to many country music stars.

The area near Orlando, Florida is home to Walt Disney World, and many other amusement parks.

Mississippi River

Frankfort
Louisville
KENTUCKY
Nashville
Little Rock
Memphis
TENNESSEE
ARKANSAS
Birmingham
Jackson
ALABAMA
Atlanta
LOUISIANA
MISSISSIPPI
Montgomery
GEORGIA
Baton Rouge
Tallahassee
New Orleans
Orlando
FLORIDA
Tampa
Gulf of Mexico
Miami

APPALACHIAN MOUNTAINS
Richmond
VIRGINIA
Raleigh
NORTH CAROLINA
Columbia
SOUTH CAROLINA
Charleston
Savannah
Jacksonville

ATLANTIC OCEAN

The South is economically, historically, and culturally a distinct region. With its warm climate and rich soil, it soon developed an economy based on export crops like cotton. These were grown on farms worked by slaves from Africa. Conflicts between the North and the South, especially over slavery, led in 1861 to the Civil War.*

In the last few decades, the South has become more industrial and urban than in the past. Some parts of the South are among the fastest-growing areas in the country. But the South also preserves its traditions— for example, its emphasis on good cooking and its slower, more hospitable way of life.

*The states shown on the map all became part of the Confederate States of America with the exception of Kentucky, which although a slave state, remained with the North.

The South Before the Civil War

A scene from *Gone With the Wind*

The South has a warm climate and a long growing season for crops. So it's not surprising that the South's economy came to depend on agriculture. By the 1820s, the South produced and exported rice, sugar, and especially, cotton. The South felt no need to develop factories. And it remained rural; New Orleans was its only large city.

Crops like cotton were best grown on plantations—large landholdings. They also required a large labor force. For this, the old South depended on slaves, who were originally brought from Africa. Slavery was the basis for the South's economy; it was also what, more than anything, made the South different from the rest of the country. (By 1820, the other states had ended slavery.)

People often think that whites in the old South lived an elegant life—something like the beginning of the famous movie *Gone With the Wind*. In fact, very few whites lived on plantations. Most whites were small farmers who did not own any slaves. But these small farmers also favored slavery; it gave them someone to look down on.

Slaves' lives differed greatly, depending on their masters. But the basic fact was that slaves had no real control over what happened to them. A husband and wife could be

The Cotton Pickers, by Winslow Homer

sold to different owners and never see each other again. Slaves often worked for long hours in the fields and received insufficient food, clothing, and shelter.

Slaves were able to survive because they developed a strong culture of their own. This culture combined African and American elements. Songs and stories, religion and community were all important.

For a long time, the North and the South each developed differently but without conflicts. The conflicts came when the nation began to expand west. Southern states said the new areas that were being settled should allow slavery; the Northern states disagreed. In the 1840s and 1850s Congress passed a series of laws that were compromises between the North and the South. In the end, the compromises failed.

Write
Many people's ideas about the Old South are influenced by *Gone With the Wind* or similar movies. Think about a movie you've seen that takes place in the United States (or in your country). What kinds of impressions and ideas about the United States (or your country) do you think the movie gives people? Do you think those impressions are accurate? Why or why not? Write several paragraphs describing and discussing the movie.

Discussion Points
- It is said that the plantation system hurt all groups in the South and that it was bad for the South's economy. How did the system hurt each of the groups mentioned? Why was it bad for the South's economy?
- How do you think songs, stories, religion, and a sense of community helped the slaves survive under harsh conditions?

The Civil War

After the fight: A Civil War battlefield

The War
The conflicts worsened, and in 1861, the Southern states seceded, or separated, from the Union and formed a new nation: the Confederate States of America. The Northern states refused to accept this. President Lincoln had not wanted war, but war became inevitable.

The American Civil War lasted four years. More Americans died in this war than in all other wars combined. Before the war, there had been great advances in weapons but few advances in medicine. Soldiers who weren't killed outright often died of their wounds. Many regiments lost over half of their men in a single battle.

The North had certain great advantages over the South. It had a larger population and most of the country's factories and banks. But it had the more difficult task—conquest rather than defense. Also, many of the nation's top military leaders were from Southern states and joined the Southern cause.

Most battles of the Civil War were fought in the South.

Effects of the War

When the war finally ended in 1865, the South had been devastated. The state of Virginia alone had been the scene of 26 major battles and over 400 smaller fights.

The most important long-term effect of the war was the end of slavery. Black Americans were made citizens and were given the right to vote.

The Civil War helped transform the nation's economy and way of life. The war effort required more factories and better transportation systems. The North became much more industrialized than before. One Northerner commented after the war, "It does not seem to me as if I were living in the country in which I was born."

Civil Rights in the South

The Rise of Segregation

The Thirteenth, Fourteenth, and Fifteenth Amendments—added to the U.S. Constitution between 1865 and 1870—ended slavery, made blacks citizens, and gave black Americans the right to vote. During the Reconstruction, a period after the war when the Southern states were under military rule, blacks voted and were elected to office. It seemed as though the former slaves might be incorporated into American life on an equal basis with other citizens.

But this did not happen. One reason was that there was no real land reform. Plantations were not broken up, and most blacks still owned no property. Many wound up working as sharecroppers—farming land for a landlord, who received a large share of the crops.

Another reason was racism. Upset by black freedom, many Southern whites argued for segregation—for the separation of blacks and whites.

Whites used violence against blacks. Lynching, or hangings committed by mobs, became common. Southern states passed laws to keep blacks from voting—for example, by imposing taxes and literacy requirements. By the early twentieth century, every Southern state also had laws enforcing segregation—blacks and whites were separated in schools, parks, trains, hospitals, and other public places.

The Civil Rights Movement

Although the civil rights movement—the struggle for equal rights for blacks—had long been in existence, it gained strength in the 1950s. Blacks had fought in World War II, and after the war many blacks had migrated from farms to cities. They were less willing to put up with unequal conditions.

The Montgomery bus boycott, in 1955, was an important event in blacks' struggle for equal treatment. Buses in Montgomery, Alabama were segregated. Whites sat in the front of the bus; blacks had to sit in the back. One day Rosa Parks, a black seamstress, was on her way home from work. The bus became crowded, and she was told to give her seat to a white man. This, too, was the law. Rosa Parks refused to give up her seat. She was arrested and fined.

Rosa Parks refused to give up her seat.

This incident angered Montgomery's black community. It was time to change the law, community leaders decided. And they thought of a strategy: They would boycott—refuse to use—the buses. Since many bus riders were blacks, this strategy was effective—and was fiercely fought by the white community. The boycott lasted for over a year. In 1956 the U.S. Supreme Court ruled that bus segregation was against the law of the United States.

One of the civil rights movement's great leaders emerged from the Montgomery boycott. The boycott had been partly organized by the then-unknown minister of Montgomery's Dexter Avenue Baptist Church, a man named Dr. Martin Luther King, Jr., who advocated nonviolent protest.

In the early 1960s there were many sit-ins, in which protestors would, for example,

Dr. Martin Luther King, Jr.

Civil rights march in the 1960s

sit at segregated lunch counters. There were also voter registration drives, in which volunteers registered people to vote. Although these civil rights efforts were nonviolent, they often met with violent responses on the part of mobs and the police. Civil rights workers were jailed, beaten, and sometimes even murdered.

By the mid-1960s the civil rights movement had gotten the attention of the nation and of Congress. Congress had passed laws making segregation illegal, making job discrimination illegal, and strengthening voting rights. The movement had achieved many of its goals.

However, King and others realized that these changes in the law were not enough. There was still much discrimination and prejudice, and blacks on average earned far less than whites. King was convinced that problems of *poverty*—of blacks and whites, in the South and in the North—had to be dealt with. In 1968, he was organizing a Poor People's Campaign. On April 4, while visiting Memphis, Tennessee to speak to striking workers, King was assassinated.

America has made great progress. But King's dream of true equality for all still has not fully come true.

Discussion Points
- The civil rights movement helped lead to major changes in the law. Yet changes in the law didn't solve all the problems faced by blacks in America. Why do you think legal changes weren't enough? What other kinds of goals have to be met?
- Martin Luther King favored use of nonviolent strategies (sit-ins, marches, etc.). Although most people in the struggle for equal rights agreed with King, some disagreed. They argued that real changes might not happen without violence. What is your opinion? Do you think violence should ever be used to bring about social change? Can you think of struggles for social change elsewhere in the world? What kinds of strategies were used?

The Mississippi River

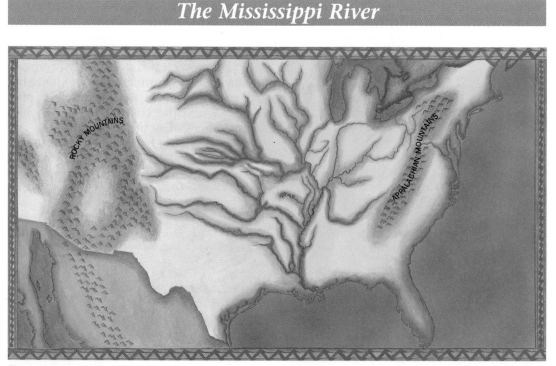

The Mississippi River and its tributaries

A luxurious steamboat interior

The Indians called it the Father of the Waters. Indeed, its name comes from the Algonkian Indian words for "big" *(michi)* "water" *(sipi)*. Sometimes it's affectionately called the Big Ditch.

The Mississippi is without doubt the most important geographic feature in the eastern United States. It runs 2,300 miles, from Minnesota to the Gulf of Mexico. At one end, bears prowl through snow; at the other, alligators lie in the sun. With its tributaries, the Mississippi drains all or part of 31 states.

Early History

Early explorers of the Mississippi mainly found disappointment. The Spaniard De Soto searched futilely for gold. The French explorers Marquette and Joliet hoped the Mississippi would be a passage to the Orient. The Frenchman La Salle, the first to travel its length, was killed by his own men.

In 1803, the United States wanted to buy New Orleans, at the mouth of the Mississippi, from the French. To everyone's surprise, Napoleon, in need of money, offered to sell all the land between the Mississippi and the Rocky Mountains. The Louisiana Purchase, as it was called, gave the United States control of the Mississippi and the ability to expand west.

Many boats soon traveled down the Mississippi, bringing cotton and other goods to New Orleans. But currents made the return trip difficult or impossible. The boats had to be pulled back by ropes tied to trees. Often their owners just destroyed them.

Steamboats

In 1811, the steamboat was introduced to the Mississippi. Skeptics said that such a large boat could never survive the Mississippi's currents, bends, sandbars, and floods. The steamboat *New Orleans* proved them all wrong, by traveling from Pittsburgh to New Orleans and back. This first trip was quite a test: On the return there was an earthquake!

Steamboats were a great success. The value of goods carried on the Mississippi increased astronomically. The steamboats became large and luxurious. They had ballrooms, pianos in ladies' cabins, velvet chairs, and marble tables.

Commerce and Memories

For a while, at the end of the 19th century, the Mississippi lost out to railroads. But today the river is more important than ever for commerce. Boats—now diesel-powered—carry bulk cargo, like oil, steel, and coal, that trains can't transport. The Mississippi is also a river of history and memories. And you can still take a steamboat from Pittsburgh to New Orleans.

Riddle

Round as an orange,
Deep as a cup,
The Mississippi River
Couldn't fill it up.
What is it?

(For the answer, see page 171.)

Mark Twain's River

No writer captured the Mississippi River better than Mark Twain. Twain knew the river well. As a boy, he almost drowned in it nine times; as a young man, he was a riverboat pilot.

Twain's *Huckleberry Finn* may be the greatest American novel ever written. It tells the adventures of Huck Finn, a runaway boy, and Jim, an escaped slave. Huck and Jim travel the Mississippi on a raft; Jim tries to reach the North.

For safety, Huck and Jim travel by night. Here are some of Huck's descriptions of life on the river:

> It was kind of solemn, drifting down the big still river, laying on our backs looking up at the stars . . . .
>
> Two or three days and nights went by; I reckon I might say they swum by, they slid along so quiet and smooth and lovely . . . .
>
> We let her [the raft] alone, and let her float wherever the current wanted her to; then we lit pipes, and dangled our legs in the water and talked about all kinds of things . . . .
>
> Sometimes we'd have that whole river all to ourselves for the longest time . . . . Once or twice of a night we would see a steamboat slipping along in the dark, and now and then she would belch a whole world of sparks up out of her chimbleys, and they would rain down in the river and look awful pretty . . . .

Answer

1. Twain tells the story in Huck's dialect.
   a. How would "Once or twice of a night" usually be said in English? What is the correct word for Huck's *chimbleys*?
   b. What is another verb for the dialect form *reckon*, used in the second paragraph?
   c. Huck tends to use adjective forms where adverbs should be used. Can you find and correct any of these forms?
2. Although Huck's language isn't very educated, it is often very descriptive and even poetic.
   a. What are some verbs Huck uses to give the feeling of moving on the river at night?
   b. Figurative language uses words to "paint" a picture or make a comparison. What figurative language is used in the second paragraph of the passage? What comparison is made there? Why does it work especially well in this passage?
3. Why do you think Twain tells the story in Huck's dialect? How do you think this passage would sound if told in more formal language?

(For answers to 1, see page 171.)

Discuss

Here's another way of traveling down the Mississippi:

The *Delta Queen* or Huck's raft?—Which would you choose for your trip on the Mississippi? Tell why.

Bourbon Street, The French Quarter

If it's lunchtime on Monday, try red beans and rice. In New Orleans this dish is a Monday tradition. On any day of the week, try boiled crawfish, which is a small and distant relative of the lobster. Just remember, there's nothing elegant about eating crawfish—often the table will be covered with newspapers! Another specialty is gumbo, eaten as a soup or on rice as a main course. The word *gumbo* comes from an African word for okra, a vegetable used to thicken gumbo.

Music and Festivals

New Orleans is where jazz and the blues really got started. You'll find there are still many jazz clubs in New Orleans, for example, on Bourbon Street in the French Quarter.

In spring you can go to the New Orleans Jazz and Heritage Festival. There you'll hear everything from fiddlers to large jazz bands, from street musicians to "big names" in music. When you get hungry, you can treat yourself to local specialties, like alligator soup and crawfish pie.

Food

When you are in New Orleans, try a café au lait (coffee with milk) with a beignet, a light pastry covered with sugar.

Café au lait and beignets

Street jazz in New Orleans

Mardi Gras parade in New Orleans

Mardi Gras (Fat Tuesday) is the city's most famous festival. It takes place the week before Lent, which is the period of fasting before Easter. There are many parades, organized by special groups, or "krewes." Even spectators dress in elaborate costumes. There have always been balls during Mardi Gras, and in recent years there is a costume contest, too. One grand-prize winner was a forty-foot crawfish!

Write

In this letter, Lucy, who is visiting New Orleans during Mardi Gras, tells her friend Maria what she saw and did. Read the letter. Then write a letter about visiting a city in your country during a major festival.

Wednesday after Mardi Gras

Dear Maria

You wouldn't believe what happened yesterday. As I look out my hotel window this morning, I'm not sure I believe it myself.

First, I went to see the parade of the krewe of Zulu. It was great! The people in the parade were in African clothes. They threw beads to the crowd and handed out painted coconuts. I almost got a coconut, but a woman pushed me aside and grabbed it. I did get some beads though!

I heard lots of marching bands and at noon saw the parade of Rex, the "King of the Carnival."

I went to the French Quarter. People threw beads from their balconies. In the streets there were men dressed as women and women dressed as men.

To get away from the crowds, I ducked into Pat O'Brien's, a bar next to Preservation Hall where I heard some great jazz a few nights ago. Guess what? Everybody was in Pat O'Brien's, too! I had a hurricane, a drink the bar is famous for. It's a combination of rum and passion fruit juice. I soon found out that although it tastes like juice, it works like rum!

To clear my head, I went to the Cafe du Monde and had café au lait and some warm beignets. The cafe overlooks the Mississippi River, and its beignets are delicious!

Then, as in Cinderella, at midnight it was all over and the crowds went home. Today it seems like Mardi Gras was just a strange but beautiful dream.

Lucy

P.S. Have you been to a good festival lately? If you have, I want to hear all about it.

Florida: America's Vacationland

Walt Disney World, near Orlando, Florida, lets you experience it all: the past, the present, the future, and world's of fantasy.

In Disney's Magic Kingdom, you can go to Main Street, USA, a town from around 1900, whose theater shows only silent movies. You can travel through space on Space Mountain, just as several astronauts have. You can, of course, also see characters from Disney movies and even have dinner at Cinderella Castle.

Disney's EPCOT Center is newer than the Magic Kingdom and technologically more advanced. Its Future World lets you explore the future of lifestyles, energy, transportation, food, production, the seas, and the world of imagination. The EPCOT World Showcase includes miniature replicas of the United States and other countries. There, you'll see everything from the Eiffel Tower to Japanese bonsai gardens.

But Florida is much more than Walt Disney World:

- At Cape Canaveral, you can go to the Kennedy Space Center and tour buildings where vehicles are assembled and astronauts are trained.

Cinderella Castle (© *The Walt Disney Company*)

- Venice is home to the Ringling Brothers and Barnum and Bailey Circus. Every year before starting out, the circus has its rehearsals there. Nearby is a college with a very special program of study—the Ringling Clown College!

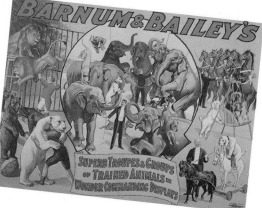

- Baseball players also "rehearse" in Florida before starting out. Many major league teams have spring training camps there. The teams play games that are just for practice. Baseball fans who are too impatient to wait until the real games begin in April can see these games in Florida in February.

- Palm Beach is the place for those who prefer polo. In general, Palm Beach is a place for the wealthy. Visitors needn't feel out of place, though—an agency provides tours in chauffeured Rolls Royces.

- St. Augustine, founded by Spaniards, is the oldest city in the United States. To go through its old section, San Augustin Antiguo, you must walk or take a horse-drawn carriage.

- Miami reflects a more recent Hispanic influence. After the Cuban Revolution, many Cubans settled in Miami. In Miami's "Little Havana," you'll see Spanish-style street lights, Cuban food, factories where cigars are rolled by hand, and even stores with signs saying "English spoken here."

- Fort Lauderdale and Daytona Beach are favorite places for college students on their spring vacation. Daytona's beach is so firm and flat that you can drive on it. In fact, it was used for car racing until the Daytona International Speedway was built.

- The Florida Keys are a series of coral and limestone islands. Key Largo, one of the islands, has a huge underwater park. You can explore this park in a glass-bottomed boat or—if you're more adventurous—by snorkeling or scuba diving. The water is crystal clear, and with its 40 types of corals and 650 species of fish, the park is well worth exploring! While some people look at tropical fish, others search for treasure. In the sixteenth and seventeenth centuries, ships returning to Spain from the New World were often sunk by storms, reefs, or pirates. It has been estimated that, along the Florida Keys, there's a shipwreck about every quarter mile!

In addition to its millions of visitors, Florida has many people who come to stay. More than half of all Floridians were born somewhere else. Florida is one of the fastest-growing states. Who are these new Floridians?

Many are retired people, especially from the Northeastern and Midwestern states. For years their jobs tied them to cold northern winters. Now they can relax in the Florida sun. In Florida there are many social clubs, apartments, and even entire communities that are only for older people. Almost 20 percent of Florida's population is 65 years or older.

But other people move to Florida precisely because of their jobs. Florida has a rapidly growing economy. From 1980 to 1985, for example, the number of jobs in Florida increased by 25 percent. Florida now produces not just oranges and grapefruit, but communications and aerospace equipment. The new jobs have brought younger families to Florida.

Role Play

Here is a map of Florida. With a partner, plan a trip itinerary. You can go anywhere you want. There are only two problems:

1. Your boss has given you only five days for vacation.
2. You have an old car, and you don't want to travel more than 500 miles while in Florida. (You can start your trip anywhere you want and must end up at the same place.)

You'll have to make some difficult choices! Use the information in the passage.

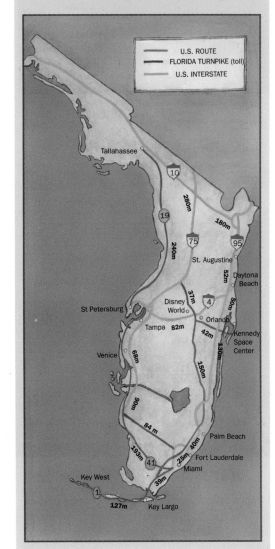

Okefenokee Swamp

Watch out for alligators!

Okefenokee is an Indian word for "land of trembling earth." The Okefenokee Swamp is in Florida and Georgia. It has islands made of peat—decayed plant matter. When stepped on, these islands seem to tremble underfoot.

Over the years, the dark, mysterious swamp provided an ideal hiding place for all sorts of people—for Indians fighting back against the whites who took their land, for escaped slaves, and for moonshiners, who made and sold alcohol illegally.

Now the Okefenokee Wildlife Refuge provides a home for many endangered animal species. Guides will take you by boat through the swamp. As you glide under moss-hung trees, you may spot alligators, 100-pound turtles, and birds that have practically vanished from the earth.

Atlanta, "Capital" of the New South

After World War II, the South, which had remained agricultural, experienced rapid industrialization and economic growth. There were many reasons for these changes. One of the most important was the invention of air-conditioning!

No city grew more than Atlanta, Georgia. People today speak of the "New South." If there is a New South, then Atlanta is surely its "capital." Atlanta has the world's second-largest airport. Of the 500 largest companies in the United States, 450 have offices in Atlanta. (One of these, Coca-Cola, is no surprise; the formula for Coca-Cola was developed over 100 years ago by a pharmacist in Atlanta!)

Another characteristic of the New South is improved relations between blacks and whites. In this sense, too, Atlanta symbolizes the New South. In 1974, Atlanta became one of the first cities in the country to elect a black man as its mayor.

With its booming economy, Atlanta attracts people from all over the country. A Californian is as likely to move to Atlanta as a Georgian is to move to California. Atlanta has also become an important cultural center not only for the south but for the world. Atlantans are proud of their city's hosting the 1996 Olympic Games.

But, as cosmopolitan as it has become, Atlanta has kept its Southern charm—its air of politeness and leisurely pace. This combination of old and new, residents say, makes their city one of the best places to live.

One of Atlanta's charming old homes.

> In 1886, Dr. John Pemberton, an Atlanta pharmacist, invented the syrup for Coca-Cola. He sold it in his pharmacy for 5 cents a glass. Sales in 1886 averaged 9 glasses a day.
>
> One hundred years have brought many changes. In 1894 Coke was for the first time sold in bottles. During World War II, bottling plants were set up in Europe, Africa, and the Pacific. More recently, Coke has introduced variations like Diet Coke and Cherry Coke.
>
> Today the Coca-Cola Company is the world's largest soft drink producer. Coca-Cola is sold in more than 160 countries.

Glossary

advocate to favor, to speak in favor of

agriculture farming

amendment a change made, especially an official change made in a legal document like the Constitution

assassinate to kill, especially to kill a politically important person

assemble to put together

astronomically greatly, in enormous amounts

ball a large party for dancing

boycott to refuse to use, buy from, or have anything to do with an organization, country, etc.

bulk large amounts

cargo goods carried by ship, train, truck, etc.

community a unified group of people; a neighborhood

compromise an agreement of a conflict in which each side gives up something it wanted

conquest the act of taking over by military force

cosmopolitan sophisticated; having people from many different places

course one of the parts of a meal **main course** the main part of a meal

courtyard an unroofed space with walls around it

devastated destroyed, ruined by violence

earthquake sudden, violent movements of the earth

emerge to come out from

expand to grow, to become larger

fantasy not real, imaginary

fast *(v)* to not eat, especially for religious reasons

firm *(adj)* hard

found *(v)* to establish, used especially for cities

futile useless, without results

glide to move quietly and smoothly

hospitable friendly and welcoming toward strangers

ideal perfect

incident an event

incorporate to bring into, to make a part of

inevitable impossible to avoid, sure to happen

insufficient not enough

league a group of teams that play games against each other **major league** in baseball, the highest level of professional teams

leisurely slow, unhurried

literacy ability to read and write

long-term not immediate; lasting for a long period of time

migrate to move from one place to another

mob a crowd, especially a crowd engaging in violence

office a position, especially political, to which a person is elected or appointed

plantation a large farm on which export crops are grown, often by workers who live there

polo a game played by riders on horseback who use sticks to hit a ball

poverty the condition of being poor

prejudice a dislike felt toward a person or group of people for no reason

racism a disliking of people and unfair treatment of them because of the race or group they belong to

regiment a military unit, usually made up of several battalions

register to sign up officially, especially as a voter or a student

rehearsal a practice before a play or other show

retired *(adj)* no longer working (used in talking abut people)

seamstress a woman who earns her living by sewing

secede to withdraw from membership of a country or organization

segregation separation, especially of a race, class, or other group

sharecropper a person who farms someone else's land in return for a share of the crops

skeptic someone who doubts the truth of a certain claim or belief

slave a person who is the property of another person **slavery** a situation in which there are slaves

snorkel *(v)* to swim underwater, with a tube that makes breathing possible

species a group of animals with similar characteristics

spectator someone who watches an event, show, etc.

strategy a plan of action

strike to refuse to work unless the employer meets certain demands (for more pay, better conditions, etc.)

swamp soft, wet land; sometimes covered with water

symbolize to stand for, to represent

transform to change greatly, to change the basic way something is

tremble to shake

tributary streams and rivers that feed a larger river

unique being the only one; different from anything else

vehicle any means of transportation (car, airplane, rocket, etc.)

wound a hurt to the body, especially occurring in war

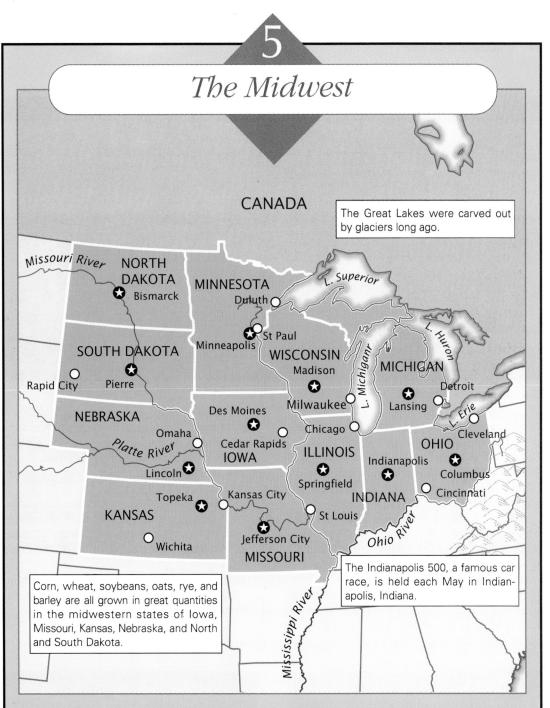

5

The Midwest

CANADA

The Great Lakes were carved out by glaciers long ago.

Missouri River

NORTH DAKOTA
★ Bismarck

MINNESOTA
Duluth ○

L. Superior

SOUTH DAKOTA
Rapid City ○
Pierre ★

St Paul
Minneapolis ★

WISCONSIN
Madison ★
Milwaukee ○

L. Michigan

MICHIGAN
Lansing ★
Detroit ○

L. Huron

NEBRASKA
Omaha ○
Lincoln ★

Platte River

Des Moines ★
Cedar Rapids ○
IOWA

Chicago ○

L. Erie
Cleveland ○

OHIO
Columbus ★
Cincinnati ○

Topeka ★
KANSAS
Wichita ○

Kansas City ○

ILLINOIS
Springfield ★

Indianapolis ★

INDIANA

St Louis ○

Jefferson City ★
MISSOURI

Ohio River

Corn, wheat, soybeans, oats, rye, and barley are all grown in great quantities in the midwestern states of Iowa, Missouri, Kansas, Nebraska, and North and South Dakota.

The Indianapolis 500, a famous car race, is held each May in Indianapolis, Indiana.

Mississippi River

The Midwest is a large, economically important region. It contains major industrial cities and much of America's farmland.

Geographically, the Midwest can be divided into three smaller regions. The northern Great Lakes area has many hills, lakes, and forests. South of that is the prairie area, which is flat and has good soil for farming. To the west is the Great Plains area, which, although also farmed, is far drier than the prairie.

The Midwest: America's Heartland

Fields of corn in the Midwest

According to an old joke, the first-prize winner on a TV game show got a one-week vacation in the Midwest while the second-prize got a two-week vacation there. Compared to other regions of the country, the Midwest has a reputation for being, well, a bit dull.

But one man's comment puts this joke into perspective. "New England is New England, the South is the South, and California is California," he said. "But the Midwest is America."

The Midwest seems less "different" than the other regions precisely because it is America's center, its heartland. It is America's center in many ways:

- The Midwest is America's geographical center. The exact middle point of the United States falls in Smith County, Kansas.
- The Midwest is the center of American agriculture and industry.
- Traditional American values are associated most strongly with the Midwest—especially with its many small towns. These values focus on family, hard work, church, and community.
- The Midwest is also in the political middle. People tend to be conservative but not extremely so.

Industry in the Midwest

A typical midwestern town

Even when it comes to accents, the Midwest is considered the "real American thing." Television and radio announcers from elsewhere in the country work hard to get rid of their regional accents and to speak English as it's spoken in the Midwest.

The Great Lakes

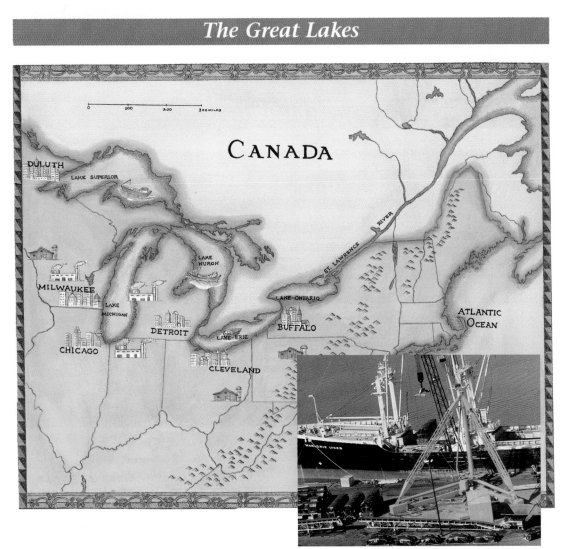

Loading cargo at a Great Lakes dock

The Great Lakes—lakes Superior, Michigan, Huron, Erie, and Ontario—are the largest concentration of fresh water in the world. They lie on the border between the United States and Canada. Of the 12 midwestern states, 6 touch on the Great Lakes (Ohio, Indiana, Illinois, Michigan, Wisconsin, and Minnesota).

The Great Lakes have always played a major role in the Midwest's economy. Many of the region's important cities—including Chicago, Detroit, Milwaukee, and Cleveland—are on the Great Lakes. The lakes are used for transporting grain, timber, ore, and other products of the Midwest.

Together, the United States and Canada built and operate the St. Lawrence Seaway, an inland waterway that can be used by large ships. Canals and rivers link Montreal, Canada to Lake Ontario and link Lake Ontario and the other Great Lakes. Goods can be transported all the way from the Atlantic Ocean to Duluth, Minnesota on the western end of Lake Superior—a distance of about 2,400 miles. The Soo Locks, canals between lakes Superior and Huron, handle more cargo than the Suez and Panama canals combined!

The Great Lakes are also used for recreation.

Chicago

Sunset over Chicago and Lake Michigan

Just as the Midwest is considered the "most American" region, Chicago, Illinois, has been called the most typically American city. And just as the Midwest is America's center, so Chicago is the center of the Midwest.

"City of the Big Shoulders"

Chicago is on Lake Michigan, and waterways (and later, railroad lines) made Chicago a natural link between the products of the Midwest and the markets of the East. Soon Chicago was a center for meatpacking and grain storage, as well as for the manufacturing of farm equipment. In this way, Chicago played a key role in the growth of the Midwest and of the United States. Not surprisingly, Chicago itself grew rapidly—from 50,000 people in 1850 to over 1 million by 1900.

In a 1916 poem, Carl Sandburg captured Chicago's importance and its energetic, hard-working spirit:

> Hog Butcher for the World,
> Tool Maker, Stacker of Wheat,
> Player with Railroads and the Nation's
>   Freight Handler;
> Stormy, husky, brawling,
> City of the Big Shoulders. . .

Chicago's Skyline

In 1871, Mrs. O'Leary's cow kicked over a lantern in a barn, starting a fire that just about destroyed Chicago. From the ashes of the Great Chicago Fire emerged that great modern innovation—the skyscraper.

Chicago needed to rebuild and could afford to do so. In the 1880s and 1890s, Chicago attracted engineers and architects from around America and Europe. These men, now known as the Chicago School, included William LeBaron Jenney, Louis Sullivan, John Root, and Frank Lloyd Wright. The traditions they began have been developed over the years by others who worked in Chicago, for example, the German architect Ludwig Mies van der Rohe.

You can see many architectural landmarks if you visit the Loop. The Loop is Chicago's downtown area (it got its name because Chicago's elevated railway makes a circle, or loop, around it). Chicago's tallest buildings are the John Hancock Tower (or "Big John," as Chicagoans call it), the Standard Oil Building ("Big Stan"), and the Sears Tower, which is the world's tallest building.

Recreation

Though miles from any ocean, Chicago is famous for its beaches. Most of the area along Lake Michigan is open to the public as beaches and parks. Depending on when you visit, you can go boating and swimming or cross-country skiing.

A game at Wrigley Field

Go to a game at Wrigley Field, home to the Chicago Cubs, and you'll see one of baseball's oldest, most traditional stadiums—and some of its most devoted fans. At other stadiums, fans who catch a home-run ball are overjoyed with their souvenir—no matter who hit it. But at Wrigley, if the ball was hit by a player on the other team, Cubs' fans throw it back onto the field in disgust!

Discussion Point

Sandburg's phrase "City of the big shoulders" has often been used to describe Chicago. What do you think Sandburg meant by this phrase?

Get It Right

You have a friend who thinks he knows a lot about Chicago, but he really doesn't. Help him out.

1. "Big Stan and Big John are two famous baseball players on the Chicago Cubs, right?"
2. "I hear that the Chicago School is a great college. Do you know anything about it?"
3. "Is it true that Chicagoans can go swimming on Lake Huron without even leaving their city?"

A beach on Lake Michigan

Abraham Lincoln

President Lincoln

Lincoln visiting soldiers

Abraham Lincoln grew up in rural Indiana and Illinois. He was a frontiersman and had all the frontiersman's skills. He could split rails—that is, cut logs so they could be used to make fences. He could tell a good story or joke and liked going to county fairs, where he'd "stand backs" with other men to see who was taller. (At 6'4'', Lincoln often won.)

But Lincoln also had ambitions. He educated himself, studied law, and became a lawyer in Springfield, Illinois. In 1834, at the age of 25, he was elected to the Illinois House of Representatives.

His political career began at a time when Americans were becoming divided over the issue of slavery. Lincoln's speeches reveal his insight and his simple eloquence. Running in 1858 for U.S. senator from Illinois, he said, quoting from the Bible: " 'A house divided against itself cannot stand.' I believe this government cannot endure, permanently half slave and half free."

Lincoln lost this election, but his "House Divided" speech brought him national recognition. In 1860 he became the Republican candidate for president. There was an unusual election with four candidates. Lincoln won,

although he had almost no support in the South. Soon Lincoln stood on the Springfield train platform, waving well-wishers good-bye. His trunks were labeled simply "A. Lincoln. White House. Washington, D.C."

Within months of Lincoln's election, the house divided against itself fell. The southern states seceded from the Union. Despite his lack of experience, Lincoln was a very capable political and military leader. He brought the country through four years of civil war.

Lincoln never lost touch with the people. He visited soldiers in hospitals and on battle-fields. He often opened the White House to ordinary citizens, meeting with them and listening to their problems.

The war greatly affected Lincoln. Friends noticed how much he had aged. Once, after a battle in which many were killed, Lincoln was telling one of his jokes, when a congress-man interrupted him, pointing out that jokes were not appropriate at such a time. Lincoln broke into tears. His body shaking, he explained that if he did not tell jokes, his sorrow became too much to bear.

As the war neared its end, Lincoln showed his compassion for those on the other side—

those who had been and would again be part of the nation. He stated clearly: "With malice toward none, with charity for all, . . . let us strive on to finish the work we are in, to bind up the nation's wounds."

Could Lincoln lead the country successfully in this process of healing? Peace would bring problems almost as difficult as war. The Southern states had to be readmitted and former slaves had to be incorporated into the society.

Unfortunately, the answer to this question would never be known. On April 14, 1865, Lincoln went to the theater to see a comedy. John Wilkes Booth, a Southern sympathizer, slipped into Lincoln's theater box and assassinated him.

All along the route as Lincoln made his final trip home to Springfield, Illinois, 7 million Americans went down to the train tracks to pay their last respects. The nation was in shock and in mourning.

Adjectives

The adjectives below are among those that were often used to describe Abraham Lincoln. (Some, but not all, are in the reading.) Match them to the definitions on the right.

1.	eloquent	a.	clumsy
2.	insightful	b.	able to understand situations
3.	compassionate	c.	clever
4.	capable	d.	expressing yourself in a powerful way
5.	shrewd	e.	having feeling and concern for others
6.	awkward	f.	having abilities
7.	ambitious	g.	having a strong desire to succeed

(For the answers, see page 171.)

Discussion Points

- One other adjective is especially associated with Lincoln: honest. Throughout his political career, Abraham Lincoln was known for his honesty. His nickname, in fact, was "Honest Abe." Do you feel honesty is an important quality in a leader? What personal qualities do you think are most important for leaders?
- The reading implies that Lincoln helped shape American history—that he helped end the Civil War and that if he hadn't been killed, the period following the war might have been different. Do you think a single leader can shape history? Why or why not?

Motor City

In 1701, Antoine de la Mothe Cadillac founded Detroit. But, in many ways, Detroit really got its start almost 200 years later. In 1896, in a workshop in Detroit, Henry Ford built a vehicle he called a Quadricycle. With this, Detroit was on its way to becoming Motor City— the city that is home to the American automobile industry.

Henry Ford

Henry Ford, a Michigan farm boy, was not the first person to build an automobile. But he

An early assembly line

Poverty and decay

Urban renewal

saw its potential importance: As he said, "Everybody wants to be somewhere he isn't." Ford's dream was to build an affordable car. Ford introduced standardization, or the idea of making all cars alike, and the assembly line, which brought the car parts to the worker. Through standardization and the assembly line, Ford was able to make his dream reality—in the shape of the Model T Ford.

Detroit's Ups and Downs

Like other American cities—but perhaps more than most—Detroit has had its problems.

The Big Three of the U.S. automobile industry—Ford, Chrysler, and General Motors—are important employers in Detroit. Together, they employ 1 in 10 of the city's workers. Not surprisingly, as the automobile industry has its ups and downs, so does the city of Detroit. The Depression of the 1930s brought hard times. So did the early 1970s, when oil prices rose, and the early 1980s, when many people bought small, high-quality imported cars. In general, when the national economy does poorly, Detroit is one of the first cities to feel it.

In the decades following World War II, many middle-class families moved away from the city. At the same time poor people from rural areas moved to the city in search of opportunity. Detroit, like many other northern cities, became poorer over this period.

Together, the two problems—a more fragile economy and a poorer population—create a huge challenge for Detroit in the years to come.

Hidden Words

Many words have words hidden inside them. Below you must find the hidden words and the words in which they are hiding. The first clue (a.) gives the smaller, hidden word; the second clue (b.) gives the bigger word.

1. af_ _ _ _able   a. a famous auto maker
                   b. what the auto maker wanted his cars to be

2. im_ _ _ _s   a. Detroit's location on the Great Lakes makes it this
                   b. these hurt Detroit in the 1980s

3. in_ _ _ _ion   a. you don't want this to happen to your car's tires
                   b. this makes prices go higher

(For the answers, see page 171.)

Wolverines and Buckeyes

Half-time during the game

The University of Michigan and Ohio State University are two large, respected midwestern schools. So, naturally, students at Michigan and Ohio State take their studies seriously—but not on the day of the Big Game. When the (University of Michigan) Wolverine and (Ohio State) Buckeye football teams meet, everyone thinks only of football. This enthusiasm isn't limited to students. The sell-out crowds include many people who graduated from the schools and many others who never even went to them!

American football did not begin in the Midwest. But a midwestern team—of the University of Notre Dame, in Indiana—helped revolutionize the game, by being the first to throw the football a lot. (Before, players just ran with the ball.) And over the years, the Big 10 Conference, a football league made up of midwestern schools, has had some of the strongest teams in the country.

Many years Michigan and Ohio State have had the top two teams in the Big 10 Conference. Often, their game together determined the winner of the conference. So it's not surprising the two schools are fierce rivals!

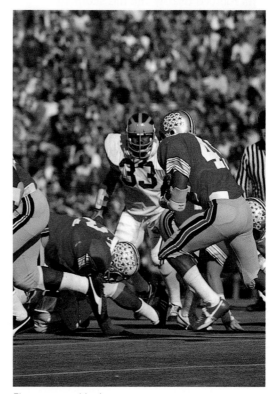

Fierce competition!

The Iowa State Fair

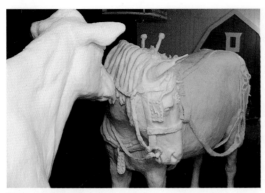

Butter sculptures

You undoubtedly know that butter is made from cows' milk, but did you know that some cows are made from butter?

Each year, at the Iowa State Fair, Norma Duffield Lyon uses butter—nearly 1/4 ton of it—to sculpt a life-size cow. The cows are so lifelike that the crowd can easily recognize which breed of cow she has sculpted.

The crowd can also see plenty of real cows—along with bulls, horses, goats, sheep, pigs, and poultry. The farm animals shown at the fair are among the area's best. The fair is intended as a "celebration of excellence."

Farmers can enter their animals in contests. Each year, for example, there are about 10 competitors in the Super Bull Contest, with the prize going to the heaviest bull.

There are many contests for people, too. You could win a prize for throwing horseshoes—or for being the man with the best pair of legs!

A prize bull

Food also plays an important part in the fair, both in contests and at vendors' stands. If you want a piece of homemade berry pie, you'll have to buy it. But you can get an ear of sweet corn for free. Iowa is, after all, the biggest corn-producing state.

Word Search

Find ten things that you would find at the Iowa State Fair. The words may be horizontal, vertical, or diagonal; some are upside down.

P	I	G	B	C	O	Z	F	A	R
O	N	R	U	R	T	O	O	F	M
R	M	W	L	R	O	O	A	A	E
F	C	B	L	D	E	H	D	N	F
C	O	W	U	T	B	T	I	R	A
R	R	O	T	T	U	D	L	O	R
M	N	R	T	B	T	W	I	C	M
E	P	N	E	S	H	E	E	P	E
R	H	O	R	S	E	C	R	N	R
S	T	S	E	T	N	O	C	W	S

(For the answers, see page 171.)

Scrambled Words

Much to the dismay of the farmers who live there, the Midwest is characterized by extremes of weather: heat, cold, rain, wind, snows, floods. Can you unscramble the weather words on the right and match them with the descriptions on the left?

1. violent, funnel-shaped windstorm   a. metudhnrtsro
2. bitter cold, high winds, deep snow   b. ontroad
3. heavy rain, loud noise, flashes of electricity   c. darlzbiz

(For the answers, see page 171.)

The Indians of the Great Plains

Mount Rushmore National Monument

In the Black Hills of South Dakota there are two huge monuments carved from mountains. One is the Mount Rushmore National Monument. It shows the faces of four American presidents: George Washington, Thomas Jefferson, Abraham Lincoln, and Theodore Roosevelt. The other is the Crazy Horse Monument. In progress since 1947, it will show the famous Sioux Indian leader on horseback. These two monuments are tributes to heroes of two cultures that clashed on the American continent. Some of the major clashes between these cultures occurred not far from the Black Hills of South Dakota.

Little Big Horn

In an 1868 treaty, the U.S. government said the Black Hills area belonged to the Indians. The Black Hills had long been sacred to the Sioux and Cheyenne tribes.

In 1874, General George Custer violated the treaty by leading his troops into the Black Hills. On his return, Custer claimed the Black Hills were filled with gold. White settlers began pouring into the area. Despite the treaty, the army did little to stop them. Instead, it moved against the Indians who tried to stop the settlers.

Crazy Horse Monument

General George Custer

The Sioux and the Cheyenne, traditionally enemies, decided it was time to join forces. They joined together under the leadership of Crazy Horse.

Custer, convinced that victory would be easy, took his men in search of the Indians. He found them at the Little Big Horn River in Montana, where they lay waiting for him in ambush. Yelling the war cry "It is a good day to die!" Crazy Horse charged. Within minutes, Custer and 250 of his men were dead.

The Destruction of the Buffalo

The struggle between the Indian tribes of the Great Plains and the U.S. army took place from 1860 to 1890. The Indians were defeated, but not just by the army.

Many Indians died from disease. Whites brought "new" diseases to which the Indians had no resistance. A smallpox epidemic in 1837, for example, almost destroyed entire tribes.

The Plains Indians were nomadic hunters: They traveled over large areas and hunted buffalo. The Indians used almost every part of the buffalo. The bones were made into tools; skins became robes and tepees; and fat was used for fuel. Buffalo meat, of course, was an important food. In the early nineteenth century, about 70 million buffalo roamed the plains.

Whites killed buffalo for their skin and for sport. They killed them in large numbers. One buffalo hunter killed 120 buffalo in just forty minutes! In 1889 there were only 550 buffalo left.

By destroying the buffalo, and changing the environment of the Great Plains, white settlers nearly destroyed the Indian way of life.

The Ghost Dance and Wounded Knee

In the 1880s, an Indian named Wovoka claimed he had a revelation from the Great Spirit. If the Indians lived in a way that was good and if they did a certain dance, great changes would come about—the buffalo would again be plentiful, the Indian dead would live, and whites would be driven from the land.

As this message spread rapidly from tribe to tribe, white settlers panicked. They were frightened by the strange "Ghost Dance." The army moved to stop any Indian uprising.

In a terrible incident at Wounded Knee, South Dakota, over 200 Sioux, including women and children, were massacred by machine-gun fire.

With the Eye of the Mind, by Frederic Remington. 1900

Preserving Traditions

After Wounded Knee, in 1890, there was little real fighting. The Indians of the plains, like other American Indians, had to face a series of questions: How should they interact with the larger society, whose culture was so different? If they did not want to assimilate, or blend with the larger society, how could they preserve their own traditions? And in view of the changes that had occurred, how could the Indians again prosper?

The tribes and the U.S. government have tried a number of approaches. But, one hundred years later, these questions remain to be answered.

Answer

1. What are the two monuments in the Black Hills of South Dakota?
2. What events caused the Battle of Little Big Horn?
3. What happened at the Battle of Little Big Horn?
4. Why were the Plains Indians hurt by the destruction of the buffalo?
5. What was the Ghost Dance?
6. Describe what happened at Wounded Knee, South Dakota in 1890.

Complete

Crazy Horse was the military leader at Little Big Horn; Sitting Bull was the political leader. To find out more about Sitting Bull, complete the paragraphs below by adding appropriate prepositions.

about	from
against	in
as	of
at	to
for	with

Sitting Bull was born ____ 1831, ____ what is today South Dakota. ____ the age ____ 14, Sitting Bull went ____ his father and other Sioux warriors to fight ____ a Crow tribe. Sitting Bull was very brave ____ the battle. His father was proud ____ him.

Sitting Bull soon had a reputation ____ bravery. He became leader ____ the Midnight Strong Hearts, a society ____ the best warriors. When the Sioux tribes came together ____ one nation, they chose Sitting Bull ____ their leader.

Sitting Bull was not surprised ____ the victory ____ Little Big Horn. Before the battle,

Sitting Bull

he had a dream. ____ this dream, white soldiers fell ____ the sky ____ the ground. ____ this reason, he was not worried ____ what would happen.

Discussion Points

• Are modern societies dependent on their environment? In what ways? Can you think of changes in the environment that might affect modern societies?
• Can you think of another example of a meeting of two cultures? How do the cultures interact? Have members of the smaller culture preserved their traditions? How?

Landmarks of the Old West

The Coming and Going of the Pony Express, by Frederic Remington

The Wild West really began in the Midwest, and you can see many of its landmarks there.

You might want to begin at a symbolic beginning—the *Gateway Arch* in St. Louis, Missouri. Located at the meeting point of the Mississippi and Missouri rivers, St. Louis was the starting point of many westward journeys. The city's role as "gateway to the west" is commemorated by the graceful steel arch, built in 1965.

Missouri was also the starting point of the *Pony Express*, which took mail to California.

The mail was taken on horseback across the vast plains and over the mountains. The Pony Express delivered the mail in 10 days—less than half the normal time. In Hanover, Kansas, you can see one of the few remaining stations of the Pony Express.

Deadwood, South Dakota was an illegal town, set up in Indian country at the time of the Black Hills gold rush. In the Deadwood cemetery, Mt. Moriah, you can see the final resting places of some famous Westerners, including Wild Bill Hickok and his companion, Calamity Jane. Wild Bill was shot to death while playing poker. To this day, his last hand—aces and eights—is known as the Dead Man's Hand.

Near North Platte, Nebraska, you can see the ranch of *William "Buffalo Bill" Cody*, whose Wild West Show toured the United States and Europe for 30 years. Buffalo Bill, who had been a buffalo hunter, was a star of the show. Others who traveled with the show included Annie Oakley, a sharpshooter since she was a young girl, and Chief Sitting Bull, a Sioux Indian leader.

Dodge City, Kansas, located on the train line, was a center for buffalo hunters and cowboys, who wanted to ship buffalo hides and cattle east. With so many buffalo hunters and

Gateway Arch in St. Louis, Missouri

Buffalo Bill   Annie Oakley

Front Street, Dodge City

cowboys, Dodge City soon earned the nickname "The Wickedest Little City in America." Its cemetery was referred to as Boot Hill, since so many died in gunfights, that is, "with their boots on." You may have seen Dodge City on the screen—it has been the setting for many TV series and movies. If you go there, you can stroll along Front Street, visit Old West museums, and even see the can-can dancers at the Long Branch Saloon.

Fort Robinson is located near Crawford, Nebraska. Crazy Horse, the Sioux leader, died there after being stabbed by a soldier. The fort, including the site of Crazy Horse's death, has been reconstructed. At Fort Robinson, you can sleep in the buildings where the soldiers lived, go horseback riding, and sit at a campfire, singing and eating real buffalo stew!

True or False
Say whether the following statements are true or false. Correct any statements that are false.

1. St. Louis has the famous Golden Gate Bridge.
2. The Pony Express went from Missouri to California.
3. The Pony Express used a train to deliver mail.
4. Wild Bill Hickok ran a famous wild west show.
5. Wild Bill Hickok is buried in "Boot Hill."
6. Dodge City got the nickname "the Wickedest Little City in America."
7. Sioux leader Crazy Horse died at Fort Robinson, in Nebraska.

Write
Write a brief scene for a Western movie or TV show set in Dodge City. Include dialogue and action. Here is an example of a possible beginning:

Scene: In front of the Long Branch Saloon.
Characters:
　Sheriff Watson
　Mr. Jones, owner of the general store
　The Kid
　Kitty, a can-can dancer at the saloon

Jones:　Hey, Sheriff! The Kid was in town. He just robbed my store!
Sheriff:　Did you see where he went?
Jones:　He rode east out of town.
Sheriff:　Round up the boys, Jones. I'll form a posse and we'll get him this time! . . .

Fort Robinson

Glossary

affect have an effect on, influence

ambition a strong desire for success

breed a kind or sort, especially of animals

buffalo a large hoofed mammal of the North American plains

candidate a person who is trying to be elected to office

capable having lots of ability

challenge something that requires full use of abilities (e.g., a job)

civil war war in which the two sides are from the same country

clash to meet in conflict

commemorate to honor (e.g. with a ceremony or an action)

compassion pity, sympathy, feeling for the suffering of others

conservative wanting things to stay as they are

contest a competition, usually for a prize

determine to decide, to be the fact that decides

disgust strong feelings of not liking something

dull not interesting

eloquence ability to speak in a way that persuades other people

employer an organization or person for which people work

energetic having lots of energy, being able to do a lot

enthusiasm excitement, great interest

environment surroundings

fan supporter or admirer (e.g., of a sports team)

football a sport in which two teams try to move a ball to their opponent's goal by running it or throwing it

frontiersman a person who lives in an area that is unsettled

goods products

graduate *(v)* to finish a program of studies at a school

grain seed from plants like wheat and corn used as food

heal to make better again after a hurt or injury

innovation something new that is introduced

insight understanding; the power of seeing the real nature of something

intend to have in mind as a purpose

key major, important

mourn to feel sorrow, especially after someone's death

naturally of course

operate to cause to work, to manage

ore rock or minerals with metals that can be extracted

panic to become suddenly frightened

plains an area of flat land

poker a card game

potential possible, capable of developing

prairie a wide area of flat land with grass but few trees

preserve to keep

reconstruct to build again

reputation the general opinion about someone or something

reveal to show, to make clear

revelation something that is revealed

revolutionize to change in important ways

rival an opponent

run (run for office) to try to be elected

sacred having a religious importance

sculpt to carve

sell-out *(n)* a game or other event to which all tickets have been sold

sharpshooter someone who shoots a gun very accurately

skill the ability to do something well

sorrow sadness

spirit a state of mind, attitude, especially positive attitude

stab to wound with a knife or other sharp weapon

stew a meal with pieces of meat and vegetables in a sauce

timber wood to be used for building

treaty a signed agreement, especially between governments

tribe a group who live in the same community, are related, or have the same language and culture, e.g., a tribe of American Indians

tribute something done to show respect and admiration

undoubtedly without any doubts, certainly

ups and downs rises and falls; good times and bad times

values things that are considered important or desirable

vast great, huge

vendor someone who sells things, especially at a stand rather than a store

violate to break (e.g., to break a treaty)

6

The Southwest

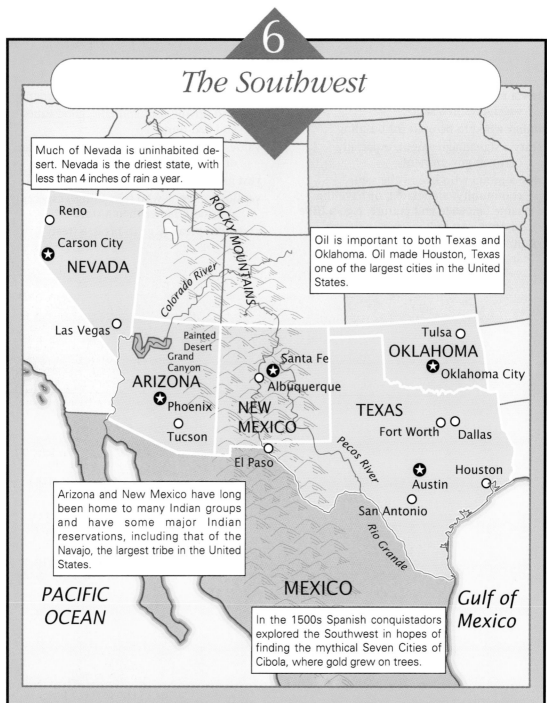

Much of Nevada is uninhabited desert. Nevada is the driest state, with less than 4 inches of rain a year.

Oil is important to both Texas and Oklahoma. Oil made Houston, Texas one of the largest cities in the United States.

Reno

Carson City
★
NEVADA

Colorado River

ROCKY MOUNTAINS

Las Vegas

Painted Desert
Grand Canyon

ARIZONA
★ Phoenix

Tucson

Santa Fe
★ Albuquerque

NEW MEXICO

El Paso

Pecos River

Tulsa
OKLAHOMA
★ Oklahoma City

TEXAS
Fort Worth Dallas

Austin ★ Houston

San Antonio

Rio Grande

Arizona and New Mexico have long been home to many Indian groups and have some major Indian reservations, including that of the Navajo, the largest tribe in the United States.

PACIFIC OCEAN

MEXICO

Gulf of Mexico

In the 1500s Spanish conquistadors explored the Southwest in hopes of finding the mythical Seven Cities of Cibola, where gold grew on trees.

The Southwest is characterized by geographical and cultural variety. Geographically, the region ranges from humid lands in eastern Texas to drier prairies in Oklahoma and Texas to mountains and deserts in Arizona and New Mexico.

Culturally, the region is home to many Indians and Hispanics, as well as the "Anglos" (i.e., other Americans). The population of the state of New Mexico, for example, is about 10 percent Indian, 40 percent Hispanic, and 50 percent "Anglo."

The southwestern states are rich in minerals. Livestock raising is also an important part of the Southwest's economy.

Farming the Great Plains

Boomers in Oklahoma on the land they claimed

"Boomers" and "Sooners"

In Oklahoma, at exactly noon on April 22, 1889, a shot rang out. Thousands of horses and carriages were off. The race had begun! This was no ordinary race. The U.S. government had promised large pieces of land to those who were first to claim them.

By nighttime, all the land had been claimed by the Oklahoma "boomers," as they were called. Some of the land had even been claimed illegally, before noon, by "sooners," who had hidden beyond the starting line. For example, an old man was found working hard in a garden of tall vegetables. When questioned, he said that he had planted only a few minutes before but that the soil was incredibly rich!

Actually, much of the land was far from rich. Like land elsewhere on the Great Plains, it lacked moisture. Many people believed that "the rains follow the plow"—that when the land was farmed, the rains would come. This optimistic idea was soon proven wrong.

The Hardships of Settlers

The life of settlers was hard. Since the plains had few trees, settlers often built their houses from sod—blocks of soil piled like bricks. The sod was difficult to break up into blocks; it had many tough roots. And sod houses were hard to keep clean!

Crops were often destroyed by nature—not just by the dry periods or storms, but also by huge numbers of insects, which would suddenly appear from nowhere. Grasshoppers could destroy an entire cornfield in less than a day!

A sod house

A dust storm hits an Oklahoma town, 1930s

The Dust Bowl

Humans were partly responsible for the worst disaster on the plains, which turned parts of Oklahoma and nine other states into a "Dust Bowl." People overused the land, stripping it of its grasses. The 1930s brought terrible heat and frequent wind storms. The winds lifted the stripped, unprotected soil and carried it for miles—sometimes as far as the Atlantic Ocean!

In desperation, many left their farms, often heading for California. This was the time of the Great Depression and there were few jobs anywhere. Others stayed behind, trying to do what they could. Farmers joked about an easy new method of planting: all you had to do was throw the seeds up at your soil as the wind blew it by!

Farming Today

Farming remains an important activity in Oklahoma. The state is a major producer of wheat. But earning a living as a small farmer is becoming more difficult. "A generation ago," one farmer was quoted as saying, "a son who wasn't smart enough to get a job in town could always farm. Now it's the other way around."

Puzzle

Every state has a nickname. Use the clues to find out Oklahoma's nickname.

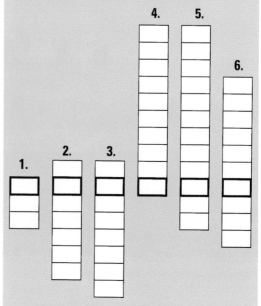

1. A building material settlers used
2. They were off when the shot rang out
3. Some land in Oklahoma lacks this
4. The Great _____
5. They destroyed crops
6. A destination for many farmers in the 1930s

(For the answer, see page 172.)

What does this name refer to? Can you explain what it means?

Write

Pretend that you are one of the family members in the picture on page 101. You have moved to the Plains from a town in the eastern part of the United States. Write a letter to a friend in that town describing your new home and activities.

Discussion Point

What does the farmer quoted in the text mean? Do small farmers in your country have difficulty earning a living? Do children of farmers often look for other work?

Texas

The word that may best explain Texas is "big." Texas is the size of all the New England states *plus* New York, Pennsylvania, Ohio, and Illinois. In fact, one Texas ranch, the King Ranch, is larger than the state of Rhode Island!

Texas also has a unique history. After becoming independent from Mexico in 1836, it was a separate country for nearly ten years. Texas was also home to the cowboy, that hero of the American West.

Texas Jokes

Not surprisingly, Texans are proud of their state—perhaps too proud. This is shown in jokes like the following, which Texans are the first to tell:

A Midwesterner is visiting Texas.
Texan: Howdy, stranger. Where are you from?
Midwesterner: Ohio.
Texan: Never heard of it. What part of Texas is it in?

A Texan is visiting New York City. The Texan is taking a taxi. He keeps telling the taxi driver about how everything in Texas is bigger and better. The driver is becoming annoyed.

Texan: Say, driver, what's that big building over there?
Driver: That's the Empire State Building.

Texan: How long did it take to build?
Driver: About ten years, I think.
Texan: Ten years! Why, in Texas, we put up buildings like that in a week. (A few minutes pass.) Driver, what are those two big towers down there?
Driver: I couldn't tell you, sir—they weren't there this morning!*

Texas Money

Texans seem to have a special talent for making money—sometimes without even trying.

In the 1890s some boys in Beaumont, Texas liked to play in a certain field where matches would burst into flames without being struck. In 1900 a man dug for oil in that field. The oil companies laughed; at the time, all known American oil deposits were in Pennsylvania. Before long, Spindletop, as the field was called, was producing over 100,000 barrels of oil a day. Today Texas produces about one-fourth of America's oil.

A Texas oil well

*To find out what they are, see page 35.

Texan Food

Food in Texas, as elsewhere in the Southwest, is strongly influenced by Mexican cooking. "Tex-Mex" food, as it's called, uses hot peppers and is very spicy.

With so many cattle ranches, it's not surprising that beef is an important ingredient in Texan cooking. In fact, the town of Athens, Texas was the birthplace of the hamburger. Texas is also famous for barbecues and chili.

In barbecues, beef or pork is cooked over flames in a spicy red sauce. (Chicken, steaks, hamburgers, lamb, or goat meat may also be barbecued; sometimes even lizard and rattlesnake meat are used!)

Chili—a mixture of beef, spices, and other ingredients like tomatoes and beans—is a Texas invention, and nearly every Texan has his or her own recipe. President Lyndon Johnson was a Texan. Here is his recipe:

President Johnson's Chili

(serves 8)

4 pounds ground beef
1 large onion
2 cloves garlic, chopped
1 teaspoon oregano*
1 teaspoon cumin seed*
6 teaspoons chili powder*
2 pounds canned tomatoes
2 cups hot water

In a large pot, brown the meat in its own fat. Add the onion and the garlic. When these seem cooked, add the other ingredients. Stir and bring to a boil. Cover and cook over low heat for 1 hour. Remove any grease from the top. Add salt if desired.

* Oregano and cumin are spices. Chili powder is made from dried chili peppers ground together with spices.

A Texan Festival

Texan festivals can be as unusual as anything else in that state. The town of Marshall, for example, has a yearly Fire Ant Roundup. At real roundups, cowboys go after cattle. At Marshall's roundup, participants chase after fierce, stinging fire ants. Whoever captures the most ants in four hours is the winner.

Marshall's festival also has a chili-making contest. The chili in this contest is especially spicy: each recipe must include at least one fire ant!

Write

Do you have a favorite meal that is typical of your country or area? Write a recipe for that meal. List the ingredients needed and the instructions for preparation. (Use imperative forms, as in the recipe here.)

San Antonio, Texas

The River Walk

San Antonio is very much a river city. True, the San Antonio River isn't much of a river; it's very narrow, only about 50 feet across. Yet it twists and winds its way through a lot of the city (these twists are the reason for its Indian nickname, "drunken-old-man-going-home-at-night"). And alongside it San Antonians have built a *Paseo del Rio*, or River Walk, shaded by trees and filled with pleasant cafes.

Many of San Antonio's numerous festivals take place at least partly on the River Walk.

Luminarias along the River Walk in San Antonio

Remember the Alamo!

The Alamo

The Alamo, which began as a mission, has a special place in Texas history. Texas, like the rest of the Southwest, was first part of the Spanish empire and then, when Mexico became independent from Spain, part of Mexico.

In 1836 settlers from the United States rebelled against Mexico. At the Alamo, 188 rebels were surrounded by a Mexican force of several thousand. The Mexicans stormed the Alamo, killing all its defenders. Several months later, shouting "Remember the Alamo," Texans won the Battle of San Jacinto and their independence.

Fiesta, held in April, includes a River Parade, as well as Mexican rodeos and other events all over town. In summer there is the *Fiesta Noche del Rio* (Party Night on the River), with Mexican and Spanish music and dances on the River Walk.

Best of all, perhaps, are the traditional Mexican Christmas festivals. At the *Fiesta de las Luminarias* (Festival of Lights), the River Walk is lit up with candles burning in paper bags.

Any evening you're at the river you'll hear lots of music, including the music of Mexican bands called *mariachis*.

The Missions

San Antonio is famous for its missions, built in the early 1700s by Spanish priests who came to convert Indians to Catholicism. The San Jose Mission was practically a town—with not just a church, but also living quarters, schools, and buildings for storing grain. The church is still used. If you're there on Sunday you can attend a mariachi mass.

The San Jose Mission

Role Play

With a partner, role play the following telephone dialogue between a travel agent and a customer. Use the information in the text and the map.

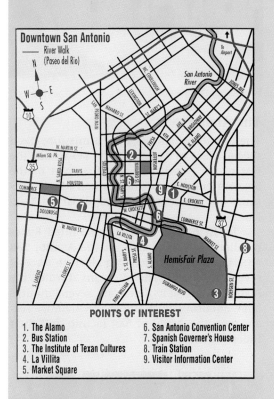

Downtown San Antonio
— River Walk (Paseo del Rio)

POINTS OF INTEREST

1. The Alamo
2. Bus Station
3. The Institute of Texan Cultures
4. La Villita
5. Market Square
6. San Antonio Convention Center
7. Spanish Governer's House
8. Train Station
9. Visitor Information Center

Agent:	Good afternoon. Texas Tours, can I help you?
Customer:	Yes. I'll be in Texas in April and would like to visit San Antonio. I won't have my car, though. Is there an airport?
Agent:	_____
Customer:	I'm not sure I want to fly. Could I take a train or bus to San Antonio?
Agent:	_____
Customer:	I've heard about the River Walk there. Is it as long as the river?
Agent:	_____
Customer:	Could you give me the name of a hotel near the River Walk?
Agent:	_____
Customer:	Are there missions to see around San Antonio?
Agent:	_____
Customer:	What about special events? Will there be any festivals while I'm there?
Agent:	_____
Customer:	_____
Agent:	No, that's not in San Antonio. It's in *Marshall,* Texas!

You work at the San Antonio Visitors Information Center (see map). People constantly come by to ask you questions. With your partner, role play short dialogues based on the passage, the map, and the information below. Start with the suggestions below to create dialogues.

- Tourist A wants to buy some Mexican crafts. He wants to know where he can go and how to get there.
- Tourist B is wondering if the Alamo is really worth seeing. She wants a brief summary of what happened at the Alamo and directions on how to get there.
- Tourist C is going to a convention at the Convention Center in HemisFair Plaza. She wants to know if there are any exhibits in the area.
- Tourist D is interested in architecture from the 1700s. He wants to know what there is to see in San Antonio.

SAN ANTONIO: OTHER ATTRACTIONS

HemisFair Plaza — large complex with many facilities (offices, restaurants, museums, etc.).

Institute of Texan Cultures — in HemisFair Plaza. Museum with exhibits relating to ethnic groups that settled Texas, re-creations of old offices, stores, etc.

La Villita — restored Village from the mid-1700s. Includes many antique stores and craft stores.

Market Square — shops, restaurants and bars, art galleries, and El Mercado ("the Market," with goods from Mexico).

Mexican Cultural Institute — in HemisFair Plaza. Part of the National University of Mexico; exhibits works by modern Mexican artists.

Spanish Governer's Palace — Spanish-style building, with courtyard and gardens, from mid-1700s; used by officials in Spanish colonial times.

The Cowboy

A classic Hollywood cowboy

People's images of the cowboy don't quite fit the reality. For example, people often think of all cowboys as white Americans. Actually, the first cowboys were Mexican; many cowboy customs began in Mexico. There were also black cowboys—often ex-slaves freed by the Civil War—and Indian cowboys. People also forget that the cowboy's main job was to take care of cows and to get them to market. The cowboy's life, although full of adventure, was hard and often boring.

Cattle Drives

In the mid-1860s, Texas cattle ranchers found that in other states, like Kansas, they could get ten times as much money for their cattle. This is how cattle drives got started. On the drives, cowboys took the cattle along trails from Texas up to Kansas and even further north.

The cattle of different owners grazed together in open grasslands. They were branded, or marked with their owner's symbol. When it was time for the drive, the cowboys would round up the cattle that had the right brand. Brands were also meant to discourage rustlers, or cattle thieves; cattle owners chose brands that would be hard to change.

On the trail, cowboys worked from before sunup to after sundown. At night they took turns guarding the cattle. One constant danger was the stampede: A change in weather or an unexpected noise was enough to make the cattle run.

The era of the cattle drive—the real era of the cowboy—lasted only about twenty years. As more land was fenced in, cattle could no longer graze freely. There were also too many cattle. By the late 1880s, some cattle trails were actually crowded!

Stampede!

Rodeos give modern cowboys a chance to show their skills. In the old days, when cowboys got bored on cattle drives, they often challenged each other in informal competitions. Soon towns had more formal competitions for cowboys. Today the Professional Rodeo Cowboys Association sponsors about 700 rodeos a year.

If you go to a rodeo you'll see events like calf roping, bull riding, and bulldogging. Bulldogging was invented by Bill Pickett, a black cowboy, as a way of stopping steers that were running wild. Pickett would ride alongside a steer, then jump on it, grab its horns, somersault across it, and pull the steer to the ground.

Texas and other western states have ranches that will take you on modern cattle drives. On a drive, you'll live like a cowboy — sleeping on the ground and eating beans and beef. You'll do work that cowboys do — rounding up and branding cattle. You won't have to do any bulldogging, though!

Modern Cowboys

Today, there are still cattle ranches and cowboys. The work in many ways remains the same. But with fences and modern machines, a lot has changed. Even cattle rustlers now use planes and helicopters!

Bull riding at the rodeo

Words

Here are some cowboy terms used in the passage. Can you give their definitions? You may already know some of these words; if not, you can probably figure them out from the passage.

cowboy
cattle rancher
round up (v); roundup (n)
cattle drive
cattle trail
brand
rustler
stampede
rodeo

Discussion Points

- What are your impressions of cowboys and cowboy life?
- In the 1870s and 1880s many adventurous young men from the east of the United States and from other countries went west to become cowboys. Would you have wanted to do this? Why or why not?

Las Vegas, Nevada

![Las Vegas lit up in neon at night]

Las Vegas lit up in neon at night

Las Vegas is a center of gambling in America. For this reason, some say the name Las Vegas comes from a mispronunciation of the phrase "lost wages." In reality, *"Las Vegas"* is Spanish for "the meadows." Early settlers were impressed by the fact that Las Vegas was an oasis of green grass in the middle of a desert.

Today Las Vegas is still an oasis—not of grass, but of neon lights. Las Vegas's hotels and gambling casinos use so much neon that Las Vegas has been nicknamed the City of Lights.

One of Las Vegas's older neon landmarks is Cowboy Vic, a giant, smiling cowboy who waves at people passing by. (Vic also used to say "Howdy, Partner," once every minute day and night. Actor Lee Marvin, in town for the filming of a Western, couldn't sleep. He

Slot machines in a casino

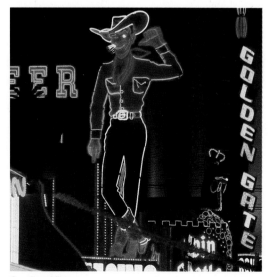

Cowboy Vic

A Vegas show

A city surrounded by desert

grabbed a bow and arrow and, leaning out the window, took careful aim. Cowboy Vic has been silent ever since.)

Cowboy Vic seems primitive compared to neon displays and special effects from recent years. For example, the Mirage, a newer hotel, has a huge lagoon that erupts in steam and flames.

Las Vegas's growth began in 1931, when the state of Nevada, in need of money, decided to allow gambling and to make divorce easy. Getting married is also easy in Nevada. Las Vegas has wedding chapels that are open 24 hours a day!

In fact, all of Las Vegas is basically open 24 hours a day. In addition to casinos, Las Vegas is famous for its shows, which often feature well-known performers.

What is Las Vegas like? Its many admirers and many critics agree that it is an "adult Disneyland," a fantasy oasis in the Nevada desert.

Puzzle

Complete sentences (1) and (2) and then use the letters of the missing words to complete the idiom in (3). What does this idiom mean?

1. Lee Marvin _ _ _ _ Cowboy Vic with a bow and arrow. (use 3 letters from this word)
2. Many people go to Las Vegas to get a _ _ _ _ _ _ _. (use 2 letters from this word)
3. What people try *not* to do in Las Vegas: lose their _ _ _ _ _

(For the answers, see page 172.)

The Grand Canyon

A university professor in the Southwest tells of a student who went on a one-day trip to the Grand Canyon. She didn't return until a week later. When asked what had happened, she answered that the Grand Canyon was so amazing that she had needed three days just to get used to it.

The Grand Canyon was formed by the mighty Colorado River cutting into a plateau in Arizona. The canyon is 277 miles long and about 1 mile deep. Because it's so deep, the top and the bottom have very different weather and vegetation. Going from the top to the bottom is somewhat like going from Canada to Mexico.

The canyon is visually stunning, with gold, pink, and purple bands of rock. Each of these bands is a stratum, or layer, of the earth's crust. Some strata took over 170 million years to form. In the Grand Canyon you can hold a rock that is 2 billion years old!

According to a Hopi Indian myth, it was through the Grand Canyon that humans entered earth. There are signs that humans lived

The canyon is large enough to be seen from outer space.

in the Grand Canyon 4000 years ago. Today the Havasupai Indians live in the canyon, in a lovely area with three waterfalls.

Early Explorations

Lieutenant Ives was one of the first non-Indians to see the canyon. He wrote, "It seems intended by nature that the Colorado River . . . shall be forever unvisited."

In 1869, John Wesley Powell became the first to explore the Grand Canyon. The rapids of the Colorado River and the narrow, twisting canyon walls were extremely dangerous. Powell set off with ten men and four boats and emerged, several weeks later, with six men and two boats.

Exploring the Grand Canyon Today

The prediction made by Lieutenant Ives couldn't have been more wrong. Today, millions visit the Grand Canyon each year. Many come only for a quick look. But for those who want to explore the canyon, there are plenty of opportunities.

You can explore the canyon by helicopter. Going up and down the canyon sides can be a lot like being on a roller-coaster.

You can hike down to the bottom of the canyon. It's a two-day round trip, and you must bring lots of water. Once there, you can stay at the Phantom Ranch, which has a campsite and dining hall. If you prefer, you can make this trip by mule.

The canyon is most colorful at sunrise and sunset. (© *Jerry Jacka, 1986*)

White-water rafting

On foot or on muleback, you can also reach the village of the Havasupai, at the west end of the canyon.

Finally, you can go rafting on the Colorado River. Because of the danger, if you want to go alone you'll need permission from the park superintendent. But you can also go with a group on a week-long rafting and camping trip. The groups use rafts that are linked together and are too big to tip over. In this way you can enjoy the rapids without risking your life.

Plurals

Notice that the plural of *stratum* is *strata*. This irregular plural ending comes from Latin, like the word *stratum* itself. There are many more common words with irregular plurals or spelling changes in the plural. Can you give the plurals for these words?

child	knife
sheep	liberty
mouse	valley
deer	fly
foot	

Discussion Point

In recent years there has been concern that national parks and landmarks have *too many* visitors. Too many visitors, it is said, make the parks feel crowded and noisy and, over the years, could even ruin them. Should countries limit visits to and activities in their natural landmarks? If so, in what ways?

Act It Out

You and a friend have stopped at the Grand Canyon for a quick look on your way to Las Vegas. You are amazed by the canyon and want to stay and explore for a week or so. Your friend wants to get to Las Vegas, where you have reservations at a luxury hotel.

How can this conflict be resolved? Using the information in the text, work with a partner to write up and act out a short scene.

Scenic Arizona and New Mexico

Arizona and New Mexico are both known for their varied and often spectacular scenery— deserts as well as mountains and high plateaus. Arizona has been the setting for many Western films, and New Mexico has been a subject for many painters.

In addition to the Grand Canyon, here are some places you might want to visit:

- At the *Saguaro National Monument* you can hike along desert trails. You'll see the tall saguaro cactus along with many other types of cactus. Saguaro cacti can be taller than eight men and weigh up to 10 tons!

- In *Monument Valley Navajo Tribal Park* you can see strange rock formations that rise straight up into the air. These formations have been sculpted by the wind.

- The wind is also responsible for the *White Sands National Monument.* The "sands" are not really sands at all, but powdered gypsum, a rock, which the wind carried from the mountains and deposited below.

- The *Painted Desert* looks like huge piles of sand painted in all the colors of the rainbow. Again the "sand" isn't really sand; it's volcanic ash. This volcanic ash preserved pine trees from long ago by petrifying them.

- In the *Petrified Forest* you'll see stone trees in beautiful reds and blues.

- Nearby but hidden underground are the *Carlsbad Caverns,* with many caves to explore. If you visit at sunset, you'll see the caves' bats (there are over 250,000 of them!) fly out together in search of food.

Write

What are four *natural* attractions that visitors to your country should see? Write a short paragraph about each.

An Arizona Ghost Town

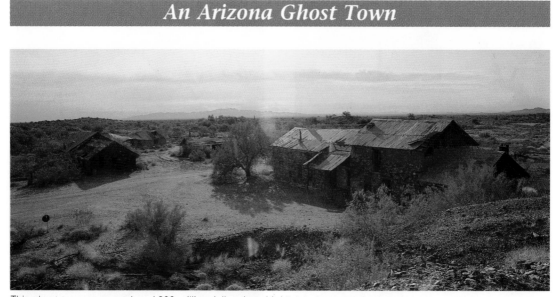

This ghost town once produced 200 million dollars in gold. (© *John Drew, 1992*)

In Arizona, as elsewhere in the Southwest in the 1800s, towns sprang up overnight when miners struck gold (or silver, or copper). When the mines were "played out," the townspeople disappeared as quickly as they had appeared. Only their buildings remained, "ghosts" for modern visitors to explore.

Every ghost town is different. Some were active only a few years, others lasted nearly a century. Some are represented today by a single ruin, others have dozens of well-preserved buildings. Arizona's most famous ghost town is Tombstone.

This town was founded by a man named Ed Schieffelin. When he said he was going to mine in Apache Indian country, people told him that he was a fool, that all he'd find there would be his own tombstone. Instead, Schieffelin found silver. Remembering what people had said, he named the town he started Tombstone.

In the 1880s, Tombstone was known for its lawlessness. After the famous shootout at the O.K. Corral, President Grover Cleveland threatened to send in the army.

People thought Tombstone would become a major town. Since Tombstone was in the desert, a company built a huge pipeline to supply the town with water. No sooner was this pipeline built than Tombstone's silver mines struck water. There was so much water that pumps couldn't keep up with it. The mines had to close. Tombstone became a ghost town.

O.K. Corral today

Discussion Points

- Some of the ghost towns in Arizona once had populations of as much as 15,000. They had hotels, opera houses, their own newspapers, and so on. Why do you think that even many large towns in this area couldn't survive?
- Some people have continued to live in or have even moved to ghost towns (or towns that are practically ghost towns). Would you want to live in a ghost town? Why or why not?

Ancient Cultures of the Southwest

There are other "ghost towns" in the Southwest—far older and more mysterious. These towns are huge dwellings that were built by Indians around 900–1200 A.D. and then suddenly abandoned.

The reason why they were abandoned is not known. Probably the climate changed, becoming even drier than it had been. This would have been a disaster since the Indians depended on farming. Or perhaps other Indians invaded from the north. In any case, when the Spaniards arrived in the 1500s the Indians of the area were living in smaller, simpler villages.

Because of the dry air of the Southwest, the ancient buildings have been preserved. You can visit many of them.

In the fascinating Navajo National Monument area (see page 113) you can visit Betatakin. This "cliff palace," as it is called, is a 135-room structure built against the back wall of a canyon. Construction took place from about 1250 to 1290, and yet by 1300 Betatakin was abandoned.

Betatakin: a "cliff palace" dwelling (© *Jerry Jacka, 1991*)

Pueblo Indians

The Pueblos include the Hopi of Arizona, the Zuni of New Mexico, and other New Mexican groups. In all, the Pueblo population totals about 30,000.

Spaniards conquered the Pueblo Indians in the 1500s. *Pueblo* is the Spanish word for "town." When the Spaniards arrived, the Pueblos farmed the land and lived in towns, in stone and adobe houses. They still do. Oraibi, a Hopi town, has been continuously inhabited since 1100.

The Pueblos have a great attachment to the land in which they have lived for so long. Many mountains, rivers, and other landmarks are considered sacred.

Pueblo ceremonies reflect this attachment to the land and the belief that humans and nature are united. They also reflect a basic

need of farmers in a dry area: many prayers are above all for rain.

Outsiders are not allowed to attend certain ceremonies but may attend many others.

A Pueblo Indian in traditional dress (*Sue Bennett/Adstock*)

A pueblo house

Pueblo women (*Jerry Seive/Adstock*)

In fact, the Zuni Pueblo believe that it would be wrong to keep outsiders from a ceremony they hold for the renewal of the world. At this ceremony 12-foot *Shalakos* emerge at sundown to dance and sing all night.

The Shalako dances are done only by the Zuni. This is not surprising, since there are great differences among the Pueblos. For example, there are seven different languages, and even people in neighboring villages might speak very different dialects.

This is the Pueblo account of what happened following the creation of the world:

Humans and animals found themselves in a dim world of running water. They traveled from this dim world, the First World, upward into the Second World, Third World, and then Fourth World. The Fourth World was a paradise, full of flowers, grass, and water. Many people wanted to stay. But they had been told to continue into the Fifth World, so they went on. After some discussion, the animals and plants decided to go with the humans, their brothers, into the Fifth World.

Getting into the Fifth World was difficult. A stone was blocking the entrance hole. The Badger People tried to dig out the stone. When this did not work, the Antelope People used their heads to push the stone away.

When they entered, the god of the Fifth World spoke: "You are welcome. But this land has little food or water. Living here won't be easy." The people chose to stay.

The Badger and Antelope People pushed the stone away.

Discussion Point

What does this myth show about (1) the values of the Pueblo people and (2) the natural environment in which they live?

Write

Myths are stories that explain the world and its many aspects. Every culture has its myths. Write a myth you are familiar with. Or, try to write your own myth about the creation of the world and/or events that followed.

Write

How did the ancient Indian cultures develop? Put these sentences in the right order so that they tell the story.

1. By about 10,000 B.C. large numbers of people had reached the Southwest.
2. All five were democratic societies and relied on agriculture despite a dry climate; people grew cotton and wove cotton clothes, and they constructed buildings with several stories.
3. Late in the Ice Age, humans came to North America from Asia, across the Bering Strait.
4. By 700 A.D. five separate cultures had evolved in the Southwest: the Anasazi ("the ancient ones"), Hohokan ("the ones who have vanished"), Sinagua, Salado, and Mogollon.

Glossary

abandon to go away from, not intending to return

activity something that people do

adobe bricks made of sun-dried earth and straw

annoyed bothered, a little angry

ant a small insect; **fire ant** an American ant with a stinger

ash the powder left after something is burned

attachment feeling close to, feeling a great liking for

band a thin strip or line, often different in color from what surrounds it

canyon a deep, narrow opening, usually with a river running through

ceremony a special act for an important occasion, e.g., for a religious occasion

conquer to defeat militarily

constant going on all the time

continuously without a break

custom a typical way of doing something

desert a dry area that lacks water or trees, often covered with sand

desperation feelings of hopelessness

disaster a terrible event

discourage to try to keep someone from doing something

divorce *(n)* the act of legally ending a marriage

dwelling a place where people live

frequent happening often

gambling playing games for money

generation a period of time about 30 years, i.e., the average period of time in which children are born, grow up, and have children

ghost the spirit of a dead person appearing to a person who is living; **ghost town** a town that has been abandoned

grasshopper a kind of insect, with long legs that are good for jumping

graze to eat growing grass

howdy a greeting used in some regions of the United States

image a mental picture or idea of something

impose to force something on others

incredibly very, so much that it's hard to believe

ingredient one of the parts of a mixture, especially of food

invade to enter an area in order to attack it

mission a building where Spaniards carried on religious work, especially that of converting Indians

moisture wetness

myth a story handed down by tradition, often telling the beginning of earth and human life, etc.

neon lights special lights, containing the gas neon, which glow brightly and are often used in signs

oasis *lit.*, in a desert, a green area with water and trees; *fig.*, something that is interesting and different from what surrounds it

optimistic hopeful

outsider someone who is not a member of the group

petrify to change into stone

pipeline a system of pipes for taking liquids or gases from one place to another

plow tool used by farmers to turn up the soil and prepare it for planting

prayer a religious meditation to give thanks, make requests, etc.

prediction a guess about what will happen in the future

ranch a large farm, especially one where cattle are raised

rapids a place in a river where the water flows quickly, often because of a steep slope

reality what is real

rebel *(v)* to fight with force, especially against a government

renewal making new again, putting new life into

rodeo a contest of cowboy skills

round trip a trip both going and coming back

sacred holy, having a religious importance and deserving great respect

special effects in movies, shows, etc., unusual, exciting sights and sounds; illusions produced with modern technology

spicy hot, having lots of spice

steer young male cattle

strip *(v)* to take off

talent an ability to do something well

tombstone a stone that marks that place where a person is buried

tough hard, not easy to cut

wages money earned for work done

7

The Rocky Mountain Region

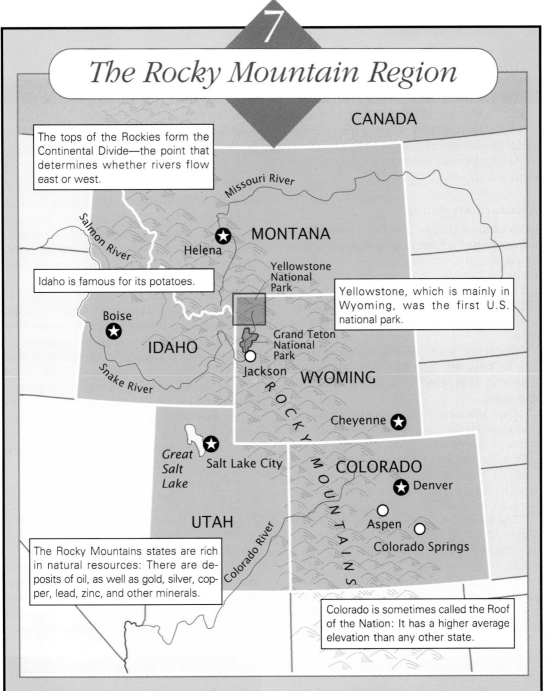

CANADA

The tops of the Rockies form the Continental Divide—the point that determines whether rivers flow east or west.

Missouri River

Salmon River

MONTANA

Helena

Idaho is famous for its potatoes.

Yellowstone National Park

Yellowstone, which is mainly in Wyoming, was the first U.S. national park.

Boise

IDAHO

Snake River

Grand Teton National Park

Jackson

WYOMING

ROCKY

Cheyenne

Great Salt Lake

Salt Lake City

MOUNTAINS

COLORADO

Denver

UTAH

Colorado River

Aspen

Colorado Springs

The Rocky Mountains states are rich in natural resources: There are deposits of oil, as well as gold, silver, copper, lead, zinc, and other minerals.

Colorado is sometimes called the Roof of the Nation: It has a higher average elevation than any other state.

The mountain region has plains and even deserts. But its main geographic feature is the Rocky Mountains. These mountains stretch from Alaska to northern Mexico and include many smaller ranges.

The Rockies are among the earth's youngest mountains. Because they are young, they are not worn down. They have steep slopes and many peaks and valleys. The mountains give the region spectacular scenery—and they limit economic development.

The region has some of the least populated states in the nation. Denver, Colorado is its only large city. The government owns much of the land—66 percent in the case of Utah.

Mining, ranching, and farming are important to the region's economy. Tourism is also important.

The Mormons and Salt Lake City

In 1830, in New York State, Joseph Smith started the Mormon church with six followers. Today there are more than 3 million Mormons worldwide.

Westward Migration

Smith claimed that an angel had guided him to some buried golden tablets. Written on the tablets, he said, was the story of how Christianity had existed long ago in America—a true Christianity, which he would reestablish. Smith's ideas made some people in the community angry. As his church grew, so did the anger.

Smith and his followers moved to Ohio, then to Missouri, and finally to Illinois. In Illinois, in 1844, Joseph Smith was murdered by a mob.

The Mormons' new leader, Brigham Young, decided to move again. After studying explorers' maps of the West, he chose a place 1,000 miles from any settlement. He led a small group of Mormons on the long, dangerous trip. The trip ended in the valley of the Great Salt Lake, in what is now the state of Utah.

The valley was nearly a desert. But Young and the Mormons set up a system of irrigation and planted crops. They made the desert bloom.

Each year, more groups of Mormons made the trip. Many people traveled the entire distance on foot, pulling carts behind them. Soon Mormons spread out from the valley of the Great Salt Lake. They started new settlements all the way from Idaho to southern California.

Early Mormon Society

Early Mormon society differed from the rest of the United States in several ways. Mormon society was largely communal. Irrigation water, for example, was owned by the community, and the church gave each family the amount it needed.

In the United States, church and government are separate. The early Mormons, however, combined the two; church leaders like Brigham Young were also political leaders.

The most noticeable difference was that Mormons practiced polygamy—men could have more than one wife. (Brigham Young had twenty-six wives.) Polygamy led to continued bad feelings between Mormons and others. Only after the Mormons gave up polygamy (1890) did Utah become a state (1896).

Salt Lake City

Today Utah has over 1.5 million people, about 70 percent of whom are Mormons. In Salt Lake City, Utah's capital, you can learn a lot about Mormon history.

The Mormon Temple, an impressive structure, took forty years to build. Only Mormons are allowed in the temple, but volunteers from the church will take you around the temple grounds. You can also visit the

Brigham Young

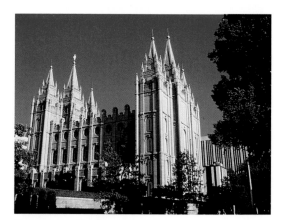

The Mormon Temple

Fun and recreation on the Great Salt Lake

Mormon Tabernacle and perhaps hear its famous choir and its organ with 11,000 pipes.

In Salt Lake City you might learn not only about Mormon history, but about your own history as well! For religious reasons, Mormons are interested in genealogies—that is, family trees. The Church Office Building has a library with birth records from around the world. The librarians, who are multilingual, will help visitors research their families.

Around Salt Lake City

The Wasatch Mountains, only minutes from Salt Lake City, have some popular ski resorts. Also nearby is the Great Salt Lake, which has water fifteen times saltier than ocean water.

The lake is a great place for floating. It's almost impossible to sink in the Great Salt Lake!

Answer
1. Who are the Mormons?
2. Why did the Mormons move west?
3. Where did Brigham Young and the Mormons he led west settle?
4. What problem did the Mormons have to solve in their new home?
5. In what ways did early Mormon society differ from American society in general?
6. What can visitors see and do in and around Salt Lake City?

Outdoors in the Rockies

Fishing, hunting, river rafting, rock climbing, hiking, skiing, bicycling, horseback riding—there's almost no end to what you can do outdoors in the Rockies.

For obvious reasons, sports like hiking and bicycling can be very challenging in the Rockies. (With bicycling, at least, there is the promise of an exciting downhill for every tough uphill!)

The mountain states have many dude ranches—that is, guest ranches for "dudes," or city folk. Some are real ranches; guests can

Mountain biking

Cowboys at work on a ranch

Hot-air balloons over the mountains

see ranch cowboys at work and can even help out. Others feature a special activity like hunting, fishing, or in some cases even hot-air ballooning!

Ski Country/USA

Colorado is sometimes called Ski Country/USA. This isn't quite fair to the other Rocky Mountain states, which also have excellent skiing. But it isn't surprising: Colorado has nearly forty resorts, many of which are internationally known. The light, dry snow is ideal for skiing.

Aspen

Aspen began in the 1880s as a silver mining town. Within a few years, it had a population of almost 10,000. But in the 1890s silver prices fell sharply. People left, and the town almost died. Then, fifty years later, a Swiss engineer built Aspen's first ski trail. Today Aspen is one of the most popular ski resorts in Colorado.

Aspen has something for everyone. Many celebrities and wealthy people have homes there. (A Saudi prince, for example, is building a mansion with twenty-seven bathrooms.) But at the same time Aspen is known for its informal and friendly atmosphere.

Aspen also has something for all levels of skiers. For experts, there are steep slopes with tricky bumps. For beginners there are easy slopes and many classes—including classes for true beginners like 18-month-old babies! Aspen even has plenty for people who don't want to ski: Dogsled rides are a favorite alternative.

There are many special events in Aspen. On Christmas Eve, people ski down the mountain at night carrying torches. Any skier can join in this unusual parade. The tradition comes from the old days, when miners working at night used torches to see their way home. The Aspen Winternationals include World Cup skiing events. The contests at the Winterskol Carnival are much less formal. They include snowshoeing and many crazy ski races.

Cross-Country Skiing

Cross-country skiing, also called ski touring, has become as popular as downhill skiing. When in Colorado, you can take a helicopter trip out to wilderness areas and go cross-country skiing there. For a more "civilized" cross-country experience, you can go on a nighttime, gourmet cross-country tour and enjoy fine skiing and fine dining.

Aspen celebrates Christmas

Ask Questions for These Answers
Most questions can be phrased in several ways. Just make sure that the form of your question fits the form of the answer.

1. Utah, Montana, Wyoming, and Idaho also have some great places for it.
2. It was founded in the 1880s.
3. Sure, they can go dogsledding.
4. No, that's at the *Winternational,* not the Winterskol Carnival.
5. You go over the countryside instead of going down slopes.

The "Mile-High City"

Denver, Colorado, the "Mile High City," is almost exactly one mile high. At this altitude, the air is thinner; breathing can be difficult until you get used to it. (Football teams coming into town to play the Denver Broncos sometimes complain they are at a disadvantage!)

Denver lies on the eastern slope of the Rockies. To its east are vast plains, to its west are the mountains. There are no other large cities around. This setting gives Denverites a sense of isolation and self-sufficiency, just as

Denver skyline

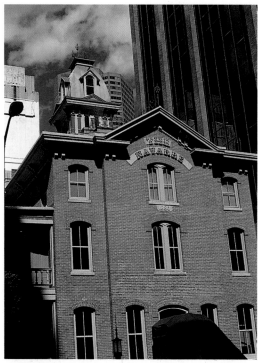

The Navarre today

in the days when Denver was a frontier mining town.

Over the last thirty years, Denver has become an important center for energy research and for high-tech industries. Many people—especially young people—have moved to Denver.

Two Denver Landmarks

The Brown Palace Hotel is a luxurious building that dates back to Denver's early days. The Navarre, right across the street, used to be a place for drinking and gambling. A secret tunnel between the buildings allowed respectable citizens to pass into the Navarre unseen!

These days the tunnel is no longer used. The Navarre is now an important museum for art of the Western states.

The Unsinkable Molly Brown

Another Denver landmark is the home of "the unsinkable Molly Brown." Daughter of a ditchdigger, Molly Brown became wealthy but, despite years of effort, was not accepted by Denver "high society." In 1912, Molly Brown

decided to sail the *Titanic* on its first voyage, because so many rich and famous people would be making the trip.

When the ill-fated ship hit the iceberg that sank it, Molly Brown didn't panic. She loaded people into lifeboats, leaving only when thrown into one herself. When the ship's officer who was in her lifeboat refused to row and moaned that the end was near, Molly Brown took charge. Wearing a fur coat under her life jacket and holding a gun in her hand, she gave orders to row. She told stories about the West and sang songs to keep people's spirits up. When rescued, she said simply, "I'm unsinkable." And, on returning to Denver, she finally received those invitations she'd always wanted!

In Other Words

Can you find the words in the passage that have the same meaning as the following words?

elegant   saved   height
independence   unlucky

Red Rocks Amphitheater

Not far from Denver there is an acoustically perfect amphitheater—a circular theater where sounds are heard loudly and clearly throughout. This theater was created by nature; it is a group of red rocks, 400 feet high. All that humans had to do was to add the stage and seats.

When it opened in 1941, Red Rocks filled with the sounds of opera and classical music. In 1964 the Beatles gave a concert there. Soon rock musicians considered the amphitheater the place to play. Today you can hear any kind of music at Red Rocks.

The amphitheater's sights are as impressive as its sounds. Spectators have a great view of Denver and can watch the sun set in the mountains.

Red Rocks amphitheater

Ask and Answer

With a partner ask and answer questions. Use information from the passage to help you form the questions from the cues below. Use the right verb forms.
Example: Why / football teams / complain / to play / Denver?

► Why do football teams complain when they play the Broncos in Denver?
► They complain because they feel they are at a disadvantage since they are not used to breathing the thin air.

1. What / the Navarre / today?   What / the Navarre / the past?
2. Why / a tunnel / the Brown Palace / the Navarre?
3. Why / Molly Brown / to sail on the *Titanic*?
4. What / Molly Brown's nickname?
5. When / the Beatles / Red Rocks?

Yellowstone National Park

For almost seventy years, no one believed the stories about Yellowstone. The first white person to explore the area was fur trapper John Colter. In 1807, when he described the hot water and steam shooting into the air and the bubbling, boiling pools of mud, people just laughed at him in disbelief. In 1869, members of a scientific expedition refused to describe what they had seen. They were afraid they would lose their reputation as scientists.

Finally, in 1871, the U.S. government sent a team, which included William Henry Jackson, a famous photographer. Jackson's photos were impressive—so impressive, in fact, that Congress voted to set the area aside as a park. Yellowstone became the first U.S. national park.

Old Faithful

A boiling mudpot

Old Faithful

Yellowstone has more thermal (hot water) activity than any other place in the world. This is caused by a hot spot deep in the earth, which sends liquid rock nearly to the surface, producing heat.

The geysers, which shoot water into the air, are especially spectacular. Yellowstone's most famous geyser is Old Faithful. Old Faithful got its name because it is so reliable: It erupts about every 70 minutes. Mudpots, another result of thermal activity, are bubbling, boiling pools of mud.

Wildlife in Yellowstone

In Yellowstone you can also see many different animals and birds. Animals at Yellowstone include grizzly bears and black bears, buffalo, elk, deer, antelope, coyotes, and lynxes.

In the late 1960s Yellowstone's bear population was becoming too large. Since the bears weren't afraid of people, they found plenty to eat by searching through the park's garbage dumps. Finally the dumps had to be closed, so that the natural balance of different kinds of animals in the park could be preserved.

The park's thermal activity also helps provide the animals with food. Heat from the geysers makes grass grow better and in winter keeps the grass from being covered by snow. Water birds that would usually fly south for the winter can stay in the park in water that doesn't freeze.

Don't feed the bears!

Jackson Hole, Wyoming

The Grand Teton Mountains

Although the Tetons are lower than many other mountain ranges in the Rockies, they are very dramatic. When they were formed, the valley floor sank. So the Tetons rise straight up from the valley, without the usual foothills.

The valley at the foot of the Tetons is called Jackson Hole. *Hole* is the word that fur trappers used for a valley surrounded by mountains. This "hole" was named after David Jackson, a trapper who explored the area.

One of the towns in Jackson Hole is also called Jackson. In the days of the Old West, Jackson was a hideout for outlaws like Butch Cassidy. Although today Jackson is more of a hangout for skiers, it still has an Old West atmosphere. Sidewalks, for example, are made of wood, as are many signs. In one of Jackson's bars, the bar stools have saddles for seats.

The nearby National Elk Refuge has the largest elk herd in North America. In 1912, when elk were starving during a particularly hard winter, townspeople raised money to buy hay for them. This is how the refuge got started. The elk at the refuge are not frightened of people, and visitors can take sleigh rides among the herd. The town square in Jackson has an arch made of antlers the elk have shed.

Butch Cassidy (center) with other outlaws.

Jackson's town square

Nouns and Verbs

Sometimes a word has unrelated noun and verb meanings. An example from the passage is *shed*. In the passage, *shed* is a verb meaning "to take off, to fall off." *Shed* is also a noun meaning "small building, often used for storage."

Can you match the noun and verb definitions below? (You might want to start by thinking of words for the noun definitions and then check the verb definitions.)

Noun	*Verb*
1. an untruth	a. to go to the bottom
2. part of a car's wheel	b. to be in a horizontal position or at rest
3. a small stick that bursts into flame	c. to fit together
4. a place to wash your face or dishes	d. to become sleepy or tired
5. land used for recreation	e. to stop a car for a while

(For the answers, see page 172.)

Words

Out can combine with other words to make new words. Do you know what these words with *out* mean? (Some of the words are used in the passage.)

hideout	outlaw
hangout	outdoors
cookout	outstanding
sellout	outgoing

Sacajawea

A statue of Sacajawea and her baby

In 1803, President Thomas Jefferson sent Merriweather Lewis and William Clark to explore the continent from the Mississippi River to the Pacific Ocean. Never before had Americans undertaken such a voyage.

An important member of the expedition was Sacajawea, a sixteen-year-old Shoshone Indian girl. Together with her husband, a French Canadian fur trapper, Sacajawea served as a guide and interpreter.

Interpreting was by no means easy. With the Tushepaw people in Idaho, for example, Lewis and Clark spoke in English to a trapper, who translated into French for Sacajawea's husband, who translated into the Minatree Indian language for Sacajawea, who translated into Shoshone, which some of the Tushepaw understood!

Sacajawea had originally come from the Rockies, so she had valuable knowledge about many things in the West. She knew, for example, which plants and berries could be eaten and which could not.

Just before joining the expedition, Sacajawea had had a baby. She carried her baby on her back on the 3,000 mile trip, unbothered by dangers like snowstorms or near-starvation in the Rockies.

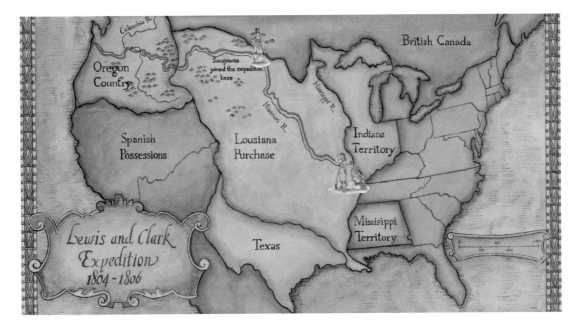

Lewis and Clark Expedition 1804-1806

Telephone

Was some of what Lewis and Clark said lost in the translation? Sometimes when a phrase is repeated by several people, even in the same language, it can change a lot in the process. To test this out, play the following game:

Sit with your classmates in a circle. One person thinks of a sentence to say and writes it down. That person then whispers the sentence to the next person in the circle, who whispers it to the next, and so on. The last person to hear the sentence says it out loud, and the sentence spoken is compared to the original sentence.

Now the last person gets to think of a new sentence.

Devil's Tower National Monument

Devil's Tower is located on the plains of Wyoming. It looks like a gigantic tree stump turned to stone. Actually, it's phonolite, a volcanic rock that rings when struck. The strangest thing about Devil's Tower is the deep vertical lines going down its sides.

The Indian name for Devil's Tower is *Mateo Teepee*, or "Bear Lodge." An Indian legend says that three girls who were picking flowers were chased by bears. The girls scrambled onto a rock, but the bears followed. To protect the girls, the Great Spirit raised the rock high into the sky. The bears tumbled off, and as they did, their claws scratched the sides of the rock.

Devil's Tower National Monument

More recently, Devil's Tower figured in another legend. For his film, *Close Encounters of the Third Kind*, director Stephen Spielberg wanted a special place for a meeting between humans and beings from another planet. Fascinated by its shape, and by the way it glows at sunrise and sunset, Spielberg chose Devil's Tower.

Write

Look at the photograph of Devil's Tower. Write your own story based on the appearance of Devil's Tower—either explaining it, like the Indian legend does, or making use of it, like Spielberg's movie does.

Devil's Tower as a movie star

A Giant Crossword Puzzle

How well do you remember what you've read? The clues for this puzzle are based on all the readings in the Rocky Mountains section. (With answers that are more than one word, do not leave a space between the words.)

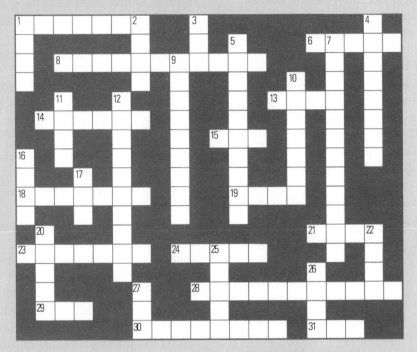

DOWN

1. _____ High City
2. Colorado is famous for its light, dry _____
3. What the Navarre now contains
4. The Beatles played here
5. Molly Brown's nickname
7. Capital of Utah
9. A member of Lewis and Clark's expedition
10. Where the secret tunnel from the Brown Palace Hotel led
11. Animal that used to eat well at Yellowstone
12. It takes skiers to Colorado wilderness
16. Went with Sacajawea on her trip
17. _____ Faithful
20. Became leader of the Mormons
22. Fur trappers' word for valley
25. Dude _____
26. Family _____ (genealogy)
27. Thermal activity at Yellowstone includes bubbling, boiling pools of _____

(For the answers, see page 172.)

ACROSS

1. Followers of religion started by Joseph Smith
6. A Colorado ski resort
8. The first National park in the United States
13. Utah's lake has a lot of _____
14. It shoots hot water into the air
15. Many people go to Colorado to _____
18. Sport at some ranches: riding in a _____
19. Devil's Tower has many of these down its sides
21. A state where the Mormons live
23. The mountains in the mountain states
24. What an Aspen skier might carry on Christmas Eve
28. One of Sacajawea's jobs
29. What Molly Brown held in her hand
30. A kind of skiing that's not cross-country
31. They were saved from starvation by the people of Jackson

Glossary

alternative one of two or more possibilities

antelope a deer-like, fast-running animal with thin legs

antlers the horns of an animal in the deer family

atmosphere the feeling in a place

ballooning going up in the air by means of a balloon

bubble (*v*) to form balls of air or gas that rise to the surface

celebrity a famous person

choir a group that sings together, especially in a church

claws pointed nails on the feet of an animal

coyote a small wolf of western North America

cross-country skiing skiing over the countryside instead of on a ski run or slope

dramatic striking in appearance

dump (*n*) a place where large amounts of garbage are put

elk a large species of deer with big antlers

erupt to burst forth

expedition a journey for exploration

fascinated extremely interested

feature characteristic, part

float (*v*) to be held on the surface of a liquid

foothills hills at the bottom of a mountain

fur trapper someone who captures animals for their fur

geyser a spring that, from time to time, sends up hot water and steam

glow (*v*) to send out a strong light

grounds the land around a building, often enclosed by walls or a fence

herd (*n*) a group of animals

hunting killing animals for food or sport

irrigation supplying water to land, usually for crops

isolation the condition of being separated from others

legend a story, especially one handed down from the past

luxurious fine and costly

lynx a kind of wildcat

originally in the beginning, at first

peak pointed top of a mountain

refuge a place that provides shelter and protection

reliable someone or something you can depend on with confidence

research (*v*) to investigate in order to get information

sleigh a sled, often pulled by a horse

slope the side of a hill or mountain

snowshoeing moving over snow on special frames that are attached to the shoes

spirits state of mind, mood

starvation extreme hunger

tablet a flat piece of rock with words cut or written on it

torch a burning piece of wood, usually carried for light

tree stump the part that remains when a tree is cut down

tunnel an underground passage

valley land in between hills or mountains

valuable having great value and worth

vertical in an up-and-down direction

wilderness wild land that is used little by humans

8

The Pacific Northwest and Alaska

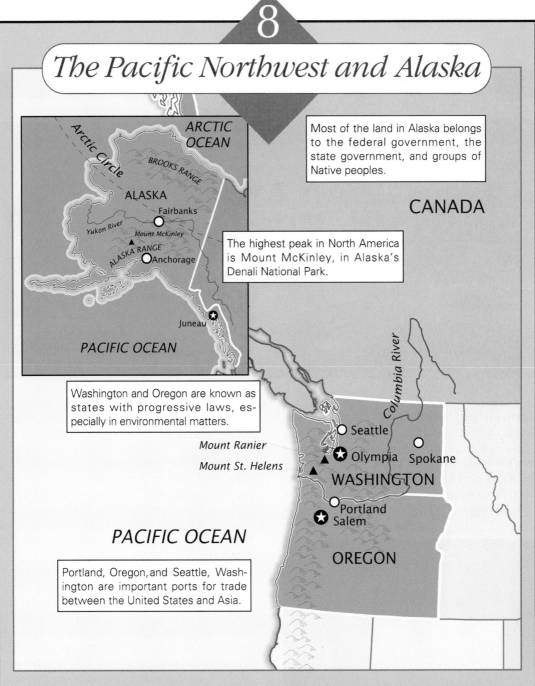

ARCTIC OCEAN

Arctic Circle

BROOKS RANGE

ALASKA

Fairbanks

Yukon River

Mount McKinley

ALASKA RANGE

Anchorage

Juneau

PACIFIC OCEAN

Most of the land in Alaska belongs to the federal government, the state government, and groups of Native peoples.

CANADA

The highest peak in North America is Mount McKinley, in Alaska's Denali National Park.

Columbia River

Washington and Oregon are known as states with progressive laws, especially in environmental matters.

Mount Ranier

Mount St. Helens

Seattle

Olympia Spokane

WASHINGTON

Portland
Salem

PACIFIC OCEAN

OREGON

Portland, Oregon, and Seattle, Washington are important ports for trade between the United States and Asia.

This region is known for its natural beauty—a beauty that is fairly tame in Oregon and Washington and much more wild in Alaska. There are mountains, forests, and rugged coastlines. The outdoors play an important role in people's lifestyles, which tend to be casual and informal.

In the economic hard times of the early 1990s, these states were among the few that were not experiencing difficulties. Alaska was doing well because of its oil, while Oregon and Washington were doing well because they are centers of trade with Asia. Manufacturing and agriculture are also important in Oregon and Washington; lumber (wood) and fishing are important to all three states.

Rain

Seattle in the rain

Rain Through the Ages

In the 1500s, the English navigator Sir Francis Drake saw enough of the Northwest coast to give his opinion of the weather: "foul, . . . with thick and stinking fogs." Three-hundred years later, the Lewis and Clark expedition (see page 128) expressed a similar opinion. "Eleven days rain and the most disagreeable time I have experienced," William Clark wrote in his journal.

And what about today? According to a joke, with so little sun and so much rain, people in Oregon don't tan—they rust. More seriously, the city of Seattle, Washington has one of the nation's highest suicide rates. Some scientists think a reason may be the rainy weather.

Not all of Washington and Oregon is rainy, however. In fact, many areas get only about 6 inches of rain all year! The Cascade Mountains run through Washington and Oregon. Moist air from the Pacific Ocean loses its moisture, as rain, by the time it passes the Cascades. So there is a "wet side" to the west of the Cascades and a "dry side" to the east.

The Olympic Rain Forest

The Olympic Rain Forest

Rain forests are usually in the tropics, near the equator. The state of Washington is more than 2,000 miles north of the tropics. But, because of the heavy rainfall, Washington, too, has a rain forest. The Olympic Rain Forest, like a tropical forest, is damp and gets very little sunlight. Unlike a tropical forest, it is cool.

Words

This passage is about rain, so it's not surprising that it has a few "rain words." Can you find three words (an adjective and two nouns) that contain "rain"? There are two sides to everything: Many words in English are made with "sun." How many of the following "sun words" do you know?

sun＿ ＿	Having lots of sun
Sun＿ ＿ ＿	Every week has one
sun＿ ＿ ＿ ＿ ＿	To lie out in the sun, for example, at the beach
sun＿ ＿ ＿ ＿	What you can get if you lie out in the sun for too long
sun＿ ＿ ＿ ＿ ＿	What the trees in a tropical forest block out
sun＿ ＿ ＿ ＿	When the sun comes up in the morning
sun＿ ＿ ＿	When the sun goes down at night
sun＿ ＿ - ＿ ＿ ＿ ＿ ＿ ＿	A fried egg that's cooked on only one side

(For the answers, see page 172.)

Discussion Points

- Have you ever lived in a place with lots of rain or bad weather? If so, did the bad weather affect the things you did and/or the way you felt?
- Do you think it's possible that constant bad weather can increase the number of suicides? Why or why not?
- What kind of climate would you prefer to live in? Why?

Volcanoes

The natural beauty of Crater Lake (© *Jerry Jacka, 1980*)

Crater Lake

Crater Lake, in Oregon, is famous for its clear, blue waters. It is also famous for the way it was formed: About 7,000 years ago, Mount Mazama, a volcano, erupted. Its walls col-lapsed, forming a basin. The basin filled with rainwater and became Crater Lake.

This long-ago volcanic eruption probably caused human deaths. Archaeologists have discovered seventy-five pairs of burned san-

Mount Rainier

Mount St. Helens before

Mount St. Helens after

dals. They are from the time of the eruption and must have belonged to early Indians.

The "Ring of Fire"

Mount Mazama is part of the Pacific Ocean's "Ring of Fire," as are 60 percent of the world's volcanoes. This ring stretches around the Pacific—from New Zealand through Japan, the states discussed here, Central America, and South America.

In Washington and Oregon, volcanoes occur as a row of isolated peaks near the Cascade Mountains. These volcanoes are important for recreation and scenery. Many climbers in the area try to climb all the volcanoes. Volcanic Mount Rainier is so familiar to the people of Seattle that they call it "the Mountain." (Sometimes they also jokingly call it "Mount Rainiest.")

Mount St. Helens

For many years, no one worried about the volcanoes; they were considered dormant. Then, on May 18, 1980, Mount St. Helens erupted.

The sky was dark with volcanic ash. Heat and wind destroyed forests. Mud flowed down, covering everything in its path. Many families saw their homes destroyed. Nearly seventy people were killed. One man was found dead in his truck, his hands clutching the steering wheel. He had died from the heat of the blast.

Mount St. Helens had been a beautiful cone-shaped mountain. The eruption flattened its top and made it almost 1,500 feet shorter. Ten years later, Mount St. Helens reminds people of the moon: It is covered with ash and huge rocks. But animals have returned, and new trees are beginning to grow.

Words

Each of the following definitions is for a word in the passage. Find the words.

1. A bowl-shaped hole in the earth
   _____
2. Sleeping, not active; often said of a volcano _____
3. A scientist who studies the remains of long-ago cultures _____
4. A sudden explosion in which something is released _____
5. Grabbing onto something tightly _____

Seattle, the Emerald City

Seattle boomed during the Alaskan gold rush of 1897.

Seattle, Washington is often called the Emerald City, or the Jewel of the Pacific Northwest. Like a beautiful jewel in an expensive ring, Seattle is in an exquisite setting: it is surrounded by green hills and the water of Puget Sound.

An Enterprising Town

At first, Seattle's circumstances did not seem too promising. Although Seattle had an excellent port, it was far from the rest of the United States. But Seattleites were enterprising: They were determined that Seattle would one day be another New York and were willing to work to make their city great. They took whatever opportunities came their way. For example, in the mid-nineteenth century, San Francisco burned down six times in less than two years. Each time, San Francisco rebuilt with wood from Seattle.

Seattleites with faith in their city were rewarded at the end of the century. The railroad finally reached Seattle, linking it to the rest of the country. Then, one day in 1897, a ship pulled into Seattle with news that gold had been discovered in Alaska. The thousands who went to Alaska left from, and came back to, Seattle. Seattle became wealthy as a result of the gold rush.

In the early part of this century, a man who wanted to make airplanes started a company in Seattle. For lack of work, the company often made furniture in its early days. Now, however, The Boeing Company has more orders for planes than it can handle.

Visiting Seattle

If you visit Seattle, you can tour a Boeing factory where jumbo jets are assembled. The building is so large that, if conditions are not

Pike Place farmer's market

To do real shopping, however, you might want to visit Pike Place Farmer's Market, the oldest open-air market in the United States. The market, which overlooks the water, has buildings that are on stilts and twist here and there. The market is also one of Seattle's liveliest places; everyone shops there. In the 1970s there was a proposal to tear down the market and put up high-rise apartments. The people of Seattle rejected this idea.

Seattle has strong ties to Asia, as is apparent from its International District (ID). Many of the people living in this neighborhood are from China, Japan, Korea, Vietnam, Cambodia, and other countries of Asia. The ID has Chinese and Japanese restaurants, a huge Japanese supermarket, an Asian-American museum, and a park named Kobe, after Seattle's Japanese sister city.

Seattle's harbor has ferries that will take you around Puget Sound. Many people actually use the ferries to commute each day to Seattle. If you have time, you can take a ferry to the beautiful city of Victoria, in British Columbia, Canada. Or you can travel through the San Juan Islands, in the northern part of the sound. There are 172 islands!

properly controlled, rain clouds can form near the roof!

To see Seattle as it used to be, take an "underground tour" at Pioneer Square. After a fire in the late nineteenth century, businesses were in a hurry to reopen. So the street level was raised and new stores were built. Under the new street, the old stores remained. You can still explore these stores.

A Livable City

Not surprisingly, Seattle has often been called America's most livable city. It's a large city,

Some people commute by car *and* ferry on Puget Sound.

with plenty of jobs and excitement; yet it also has a small-town atmosphere, with friendly people. It has fine theaters, and yet it also has water and mountains.

Seattleites no longer wish their city were more like New York. Ironically, it is in danger of becoming so.

Limits to Growth?

In the 1980s, the word spread that Seattle was *the* place to live. People began moving to Seattle—from the East Coast, from the Midwest, and especially from California. They wanted to get away from traffic, crowds, pollution, and crime.

Soon Seattle's prices increased dramatically. Crowds, pollution, and crime also increased. The new slogan in Seattle became "Have a nice day—somewhere else." Instead of defending their city when outsiders complained about its rain, Seattleites began to exaggerate about how much rain there was.

How can a city handle growth? This is the question Seattle must now deal with.

Match

Match each of the following places with the phrase that best describes it.

1. the ID	a. Rain clouds could form here
2. Seattle	b. A place with underground tours
3. Puget Sound	c. A place to shop
4. the Boeing factory	d. The Emerald City
5. Pioneer Square	e. A place to travel by ferry
6. Pike Place Farmer's Market	f. Seattle's Asian influences are obvious here

True or False

Indicate whether the statements are true or false. Correct any statements that are false.

1. Seattle is a port city.
2. Seattle is located in the state of Oregon.
3. Seattle became wealthy when gold was found there.
4. Many planes are built in Seattle.
5. Seattle has strong ties to Europe.
6. Seattleites are worried that their city is not growing enough.

(For the answers to both exercises, see page 172.)

Discussion Points

- In your opinion, what things make a city liveable? Based on the passage, do you think you would want to live in Seattle? Why or why not?
- Are there certain cities in your country that many people want to move to? Do these cities have problems with growth? If so, what kinds of problems?
- How do you think Seattle—or other cities—can handle growth?

The Abundance of the Pacific Northwest

The Pacific Northwest has an abundance of natural resources. From the time of the Indians, this abundance has shaped the way people live there.

A totem pole

The Potlatch

The Indians of the Pacific Northwest coast had plenty to eat: animals, berries, and salmon and other fish. The tall cedar trees were another important resource. The Indians used cedar for houses and even for clothes. They also used cedar to make totem poles.

Totem poles are tall poles on which figures are carved and painted. The figures tell a story, often about a person's ancestors. This beautiful and complex art form could develop because of the abundance of the Pacific Northwest. As food was easily obtained, there was time for leisure.

Abundance also made possible the most unusual aspect of Pacific Northwest Indian culture: the potlatch, or gift-giving ceremony. The host of a potlatch invited hundreds of guests to a great feast. At the feast, the host gave everyone gifts. The greatness of the gifts showed the host's wealth and power. The guests then had to invite the host to a potlatch with even greater gifts.

Trapping, Mining, Logging

The first whites who came to the Pacific Northwest came looking for something the region did *not* have: a "Northwest Passage," or sea route joining Europe and Asia. They found otters and other animals whose furs were highly valued in China. This fur trade brought Russians, British, and Americans to the area.

As more animals were killed, fur trapping and trading became less profitable. Settlers turned increasingly to the region's other resources: land, fish, and trees.

With new techniques, fishing and logging soon became very efficient—too efficient. One area in the state of Washington, for example, cut down 90 percent of its vast forests in less than ten years!

The Situation Today

The Pacific Northwest still has abundant resources, and these resources still make pos-

Loggers cut down vast forests

sible a good way of life. But the Pacific Northwest cannot just use up its resources. So, the region has been diversifying its economy, to avoid depending on logging and fishing.

High-technology manufacturing has become important. So has trade with the Far East, especially with Japan. Ports in Washington and Oregon handle one-quarter of all trade between the United States and the Far East. Farming, including grape cultivation, has also become more important. In 1975 there were fewer than 10 wineries in Washington and Oregon; now there are over 150.

Cargo ships being loaded in Seattle

Answer

1. What is a totem pole?
2. What is the potlatch and how did abundance make it possible?
3. What are some of the resources the Pacific Northwest has an abundance of?
4. What did the first whites in the area do?
5. The passage says that fishing and logging became *too* efficient. What does this mean?
6. Why is the region trying to diversify its economy?
7. What are some of the economic activities in the Pacific Northwest today?

Alaska: Land and People

Alaska is different, and Alaskans know it. They refer to the other states as "Outside" or the "Lower 48."*

Alaska is big. It is twice the size of Texas, the next-largest state, and almost one-fourth the size of the Lower 48. Alaska spans four time zones.

Alaska's location, of course, also makes it different. One-third of Alaska is above the Arctic Circle. Areas near the Arctic Circle experience long periods of perpetual light in summer and long periods of perpetual dark in winter. Alaska has had temperatures as low as −80°F and has areas of permafrost, ground that is always frozen. Parts of Alaska are so remote that many mountains there have not yet been named!

Although Alaska is the largest state, it has the fewest people: 0.7 persons per square mile. (If Manhattan had this population density, it would have only 14 people!)

---

*The "Lower 48" refers only to the continental United States; it doesn't include Hawaii.

Alaska has green forests...

...and glaciers.

According to an Indian legend, an Indian long ago helped a giant in Siberia kill his rival, who fell dead into the sea, forming a land bridge to North America. Scientists say that at times from about 15,000 to about 40,000 years ago, the sea level was so low that people could walk from Siberia to North America. These were the first inhabitants in the Americas. Some stayed in Alaska; others, over thousands of years, migrated south and east.

Today Alaska has slightly over 500,000 people, about 15 percent of whom are native. "Native" refers to people in three groups: Indian, Eskimo, and Aleut. The Indians are of several different tribes. The Eskimo live not only in Alaska but in an area from Siberia to Greenland. The origin of the Aleuts is not known. It is thought they may have come long ago from a northern island of Japan.

The first non-Natives came from Russia. Many Alaskans still belong to the Russian Orthodox church. Since the 1950s, the number of non-Natives has increased greatly.

Among non-Natives there are many more men than women. One woman started a magazine where Alaskan men looking for wives could put a picture of themselves along with a brief description. Responses from women have literally come from around the world—one response was from Antarctica!

Find Questions for These Answers

Ask questions appropriate for these answers. More than one question may be appropriate.

1. From 15,000 to 40,000 years ago.
2. From Siberia.
3. Indians, Aleuts, and Eskimo.
4. "Outside" or "the Lower 48."
5. It has the most of all of the states.
6. It has the least of all of the states.
7. More men.

Figuratively Speaking

The passage says that responses to the magazine "have literally come from around the world." The word "literally" is used because "from around the world" is usually a figure of speech, meaning "from many places," but here is used literally, since Antarctica is around the world from the Arctic.

Figures of speech are common (although many would make no sense if used literally!). Do you know what the figures of speech in these sentences mean?

1. He was *as hungry as a bear.*
2. She gave him *a look that could kill.*
3. He *cried his eyes out.*
4. She told him she wouldn't speak to him *until hell froze over.*

How else could these sentences be stated in English? Does your language have figures of speech that could be used in these contexts?

Traveling in Alaska

Dogsled racing in Alaska

Traditionally, Eskimos used dogsleds to get around in winter. Now, snowmobiles have largely replaced dogsleds. But dogsled racing is a favorite Alaskan sport. And if you go to Alaska, you can take a dogsled tour. On a dog- sled or otherwise, travel in Alaska is unusual and interesting.

Alaska has only about 10,000 miles of road—not much, especially for a state its size. The Alaska Highway (Alcan) links Alaska to

Four Alaskan animals: Kodiak bear, moose, musk ox, caribou

the other states through Canada. Traveling on the Alcan used to be very rough. Now, however, the Alcan is fully paved and has gas stations every 50 miles. On Alaskan roads you are almost as likely to see an animal—say, a bear or a moose—as you are to see another car.

In Southeast and South Central Alaska, you're best off traveling on the Maritime Highway, which isn't a road at all, but a system of ferries. Because of geography, travel by water in these areas is much easier than travel by road. In fact, only three cities in the Southeast can be reached by road. The others, in-

Many places in Alaska can only be reached by ferry.

An Alaskan bush plane takes off.

cluding Juneau, Alaska's capital, can be reached only by water or air.

In many ways, air travel is the most important form of transportation. Almost every community in Alaska has a landing field for planes. "Bush planes" fly to Alaska's small, distant communities. They are propeller driven and can land on floats or skis. Bush pilots are heroes in Alaska—and rightly so. They often fly under extremely dangerous conditions.

Look and Practice

With a partner, use the map of Alaska to ask and answer questions about travel in Alaska. Use the following examples to start.

A: Can I go by highway from Fairbanks to Nome?
B: No, you'll have to take a plane.
A: Where does the train from Seward end?
B: It ends in Fairbanks.

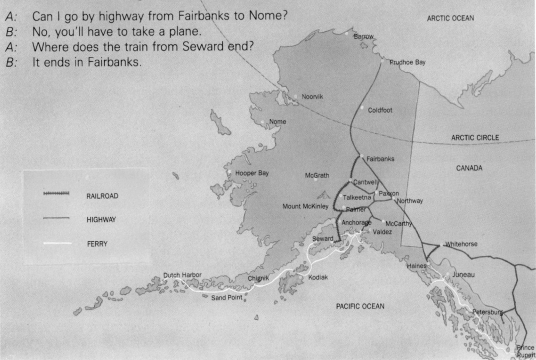

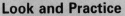

The Regions of Alaska

The city of Juneau is dwarfed by mountains.

Alaska has five major regions: the Southeast, South Central, Interior, Southwest, and Arctic regions.

Southeast Alaska

The Southeast consists of a thin strip of mainland and islands. It is a magnificently scenic land of ocean, rugged coasts, steep mountains, glaciers, and rainforests.

Sitka, a Southeast fishing town, was the center of Alaska in the days when Alaska was Russian. In 1867, Russia sold Alaska to the United States, in a treaty signed by Secretary of State William Seward. The purchase price amounted to only 2 cents per acre, yet many Americans thought the purchase so foolish that they called it "Seward's Folly" and called Alaska "Seward's Icebox." When Alaska's natural wealth became apparent, these names soon disappeared.

Juneau, Alaska's capital, is larger in area than any other city in the United States but has only about 25,000 residents. Juneau began in the 1880s as a gold-mining town, and some of its buildings still preserve this frontier character. Parts of the city are so steep that there are wooden stairs instead of sidewalks.

South Central Alaska

South Central Alaska, a mainly coastal area, has over half of Alaska's population. The majority of these people live in the city of Anchorage.

Anchorage is Alaska's most heavily populated city, and Alaskans tend to either love it or hate it. Those who love Anchorage point to its sophistication. So do those who hate it; they jokingly say that the only good thing about Anchorage is that it's "just a plane trip away from Alaska."

True, Anchorage is largely new. In 1964 this part of Alaska was hit by a strong earthquake; much of Anchorage had to be rebuilt. Also, Anchorage has grown rapidly since the

Anchorage

1970s, when it became the center for Alaska's booming oil industry. But in Anchorage the new high-rise buildings are mixed in with houses and even cabins. A reporter who was recently in Anchorage told of traffic being held up following a collision—between a car and a moose!

Palmer is an agricultural town in a state with little agriculture. Although the summer growing season is short, summer days have as many as 20 hours of daylight. The result is giant-sized fruits and vegetables—strawberries larger than eggs and 75-pound cabbages!

The town of **Talkeetna** is a starting-point for expeditions climbing Mount McKinley, North America's tallest mountain. Bush pilots in Talkeetna are experts in landing on glaciers.

The Interior

The Interior is a vast plateau between two mountain ranges. It has thick forests but also areas of permafrost. Winter temperatures of −60°F are not uncommon and yet summer temperatures have reached 90°F.

Fairbanks was founded in 1901 almost by accident. A man named Barnette was traveling upriver to start a trading post further north. Travel became difficult, and the boat's captain refused to continue. As he and Barnette were arguing, a man suddenly appeared. He said he had found gold nearby but was out of supplies. Barnette gladly got off the boat with his supplies. All three men were happy, and Fairbanks was born.

Fairbanks is Alaska's second-largest city. It is near the Arctic Circle—one of the few cities in the world that is so far north.

An oversized cabbage from Palmer

Hikers approach Mt. McKinley.

Fishing off the Aleutian Islands

Southwest Alaska

Southwest Alaska consists of a peninsula—the Alaska Peninsula—and islands, including the Aleutian Islands, which reach out over one thousand miles into the Pacific. The relatively few people who live in the Southwest are mainly Aleut and Eskimo. Except for its forested western part, the Southwest is tundra, land without trees. The weather tends to be foggy, rainy, and windy.

The Arctic Region

There are small, scattered settlements on the western and northern Arctic coasts. Much of the Arctic region is north of the Brooks Range, mountains that may be the emptiest, least-explored wilderness in the world.

Nome got its name by mistake. An early mapmaker, uncertain as to whether the area had a name, wrote "Name" with a question mark on his map. His "Name" was later misread as "Nome."

Nome became known when gold was discovered on its beaches. In no time, its population grew from under 300 to over 30,000. Today Nome has about 2,500 people, most of whom are Natives.

Barrow is on the northern coast and has a population of 3,000. At Barrow you can walk off the edge of North America into the Arctic Ocean, which is frozen 11 months of the year. Because of its location, Barrow has 84 days in summer during which the sun never sets and an equal number of days in winter during which it never rises.

Ask and Answer

With a partner, ask and answer questions using the cues below. Then ask and answer other questions about the regions of Alaska.

1. What / the capital / Alaska?
2. What / the largest city / Alaska?
3. Why / purchase / Alaska / call / Seward's Folly?
4. What country / the United States / purchase / Alaska?
5. How / Nome / its name?

Alaskan Land Use

Alaskan land is incredibly beautiful. It is also very rich in natural resources. One-fifth of all oil produced in the United States is from Alaska.

The Basic Debate

Since Alaska became a state in 1959, there has been controversy over how the land should be used.

Those on one side of the controversy argue that Alaska is America's last frontier. Only Alaska has undisturbed land—land that is much like it was hundreds of years ago. The land should be kept that way, for future generations to enjoy.

Those on the other side argue that Alaskans benefit economically from development

The Alaskan pipeline

and use of the land. They point to oil as an example.

Oil

In most states people pay money to the state government in the form of taxes; Alaskans *get* money *from* their state government. The reason is oil.

In the late 1960s oil was discovered in Prudhoe Bay on the Arctic Ocean. By the mid-1970s the pipeline to Valdez, in south-central Alaska, had been built and the oil began to flow. Within a couple of years, 85 percent of Alaska's money was coming from oil. Each year, the state government saves some of this money, uses some for schools, roads, and so forth, and gives a small amount to all residents of Alaska.

However, by the year 2000, the oil from Prudhoe Bay will probably be only about half the amount it was in 1990. Oil companies have found oil off the coast of the Arctic National Wildlife Refuge and hope to begin drilling there.

Conservationists say that drilling should not be undertaken. They point out that the Arctic Refuge is an unusual and fragile environment. They also argue that at the rate that Americans consume oil, this new oil would not help for long. The real solution, they say, is for Americans to use less oil.

The Exxon Valdez

In March 1989, the oil tanker Exxon *Valdez* hit a rock off the southern coast of Alaska and

Development can also lead to disaster.

leaked 11 million gallons of oil. Many miles of beach were affected; many fish, birds, and animals died. Scientists cannot yet determine the full effects of this huge oil spill.

One effect of the spill was to strengthen—at least for the moment—the position of conservationists who oppose more drilling. But the debate is by no means over.

Debate

For purposes of discussing future oil exploration and drilling in Alaska, choose to be either an oil company executive or a conservationist.

Read through the passage and make a list of reasons why, from your point of view, there should or should not be new drilling at the Arctic Refuge and other Alaskan sites. Can you think of any other arguments to support your position? Write these down, too. Then get together with other students who have chosen your position and prepare for a debate.

Some students can, instead of taking either side, be the decision makers. They can ask questions of both sides and, when the debate is over, can vote on whether or not there should be new drilling.

Glossary

abundance a great plenty

basin a hollow place where water collects

benefit *(v)* to help out; to be helped out

casual relaxed, informal

circumstances the conditions connected with something

commute to travel to and from work

complex not simple

consume to use up

controversy an argument between sides with opposite views

damp moist; having moist air

debate a discussion of arguments that are made by two sides with different views

determined feeling strongly about doing something

disagreeable unpleasant

diversify to make more varied

dogsled a sled drawn by dogs

drill to make a hole in a hard substance

efficient able to get a job done well

emerald a green precious stone

enterprising being energetic and ready to do what is needed, including things that are different and new

exaggerate to overstate something, making it seem larger (or worse, better, etc.) than it really is

expert a person with special knowledge about some subject

exquisite of great excellence, or quality

faith trust, confidence

ferry a boat that carries people and things across a river or other body of water

folly something foolish

fragile delicate, easily destroyed

glacier a slowly moving mass of ice that is formed from packed snow

handle *(v)* to deal with

inhabitant someone who lives in a place

leisure time not spent working

lifestyle a typical way of living

livable the quality of being a good place to live

logging cutting down trees for their wood

natural resources a source of wealth that occurs in nature (minerals, trees, etc.)

otter a fur-covered water animal

perpetual going on without stopping

plateau a large area of level land higher than the land that surrounds it

pollution dirt in air, water, etc.; especially dirt caused by human activities

propeller a device with two or more blades to move a helicopter, airplane, etc.

purchase (*n*) something that is bought; (*v*) to buy something

rain forest an area with heavy rainfall and many trees

recreation amusement; activities done for fun, in contrast to work

reject to refuse, to say "no" to

remote far away from anything

rust (*v*) (for a metal) to become covered with a reddish-brown coating as a result of moisture

salmon a large fish, generally with pink flesh

sandals a kind of a shoe made of a bottom piece and straps

scattered spread out in different places

setting surroundings; for a jewel, the metal in which it is fixed

snowmobile a motorized vehicle for travel on snow

sophistication not being simple, having culture (used for a person, a city, etc.)

sound (*n*) a narrow passage of water joining two larger areas of water

steering wheel wheel used to control the direction of a car

stilts poles

suicide the act of killing oneself

tame (*adj*) not wild, easily controlled

tan (*v*) to become brown in the sun

technique a method, a way of doing something

trading post a store in an area without many people, whose owner sells or trades supplies

willing ready to do what is needed

winery a place where wine is made

9

California and Hawaii

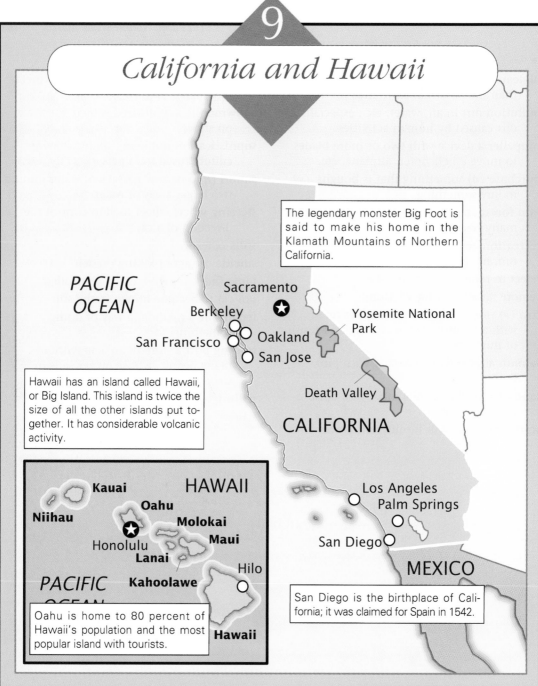

PACIFIC OCEAN

The legendary monster Big Foot is said to make his home in the Klamath Mountains of Northern California.

Sacramento ★

Berkeley

Oakland

San Francisco

San Jose

Yosemite National Park

Death Valley

CALIFORNIA

Hawaii has an island called Hawaii, or Big Island. This island is twice the size of all the other islands put together. It has considerable volcanic activity.

HAWAII

Kauai

Oahu

Niihau

Molokai

Honolulu ★

Maui

Lanai

Kahoolawe

Hilo

PACIFIC OCEAN

Oahu is home to 80 percent of Hawaii's population and the most popular island with tourists.

Hawaii

Los Angeles

Palm Springs

San Diego

MEXICO

San Diego is the birthplace of California; it was claimed for Spain in 1542.

These two states are grouped together mainly because they are relatively near each other: California, although 2,500 miles from Hawaii, is the closest state to Hawaii. California is the most populated of the states and one of the largest. The eight islands of Hawaii are together one of the smallest, least populated states. The two states do have a few things in common: culturally diverse populations, and lots of sun and sand.

California

The beautiful coastline of northern California

California is frequently described as being "like America, only more so." In California, America's good points often seem even better and its problems even worse. Many people think of California as the state that symbolizes the American dream. There, individuals have the opportunity to succeed—to do and be what they want.

Geography adds to the sense that California is somehow a symbol of the American dream. When you stand on California's high, rocky northern coast, you are aware that you are at the end of the continent. For several centuries, Americans pushed west in search of a better life. California was as far as they could go.

But just what is California like? This question is hard to answer because California is, above all, diverse: In a way, there are many Californias.

Land

Obviously, the rocky coast of the north is very different from the sandy beaches for which southern California is famous. California also has many other different environments. Here are two examples:

Redwood trees grow in only two places: a small area in China and an area in northern California. The redwoods are very tall; a park

A stand of Redwoods

Death Valley, lowest spot in the U.S.

in California has three of the world's six tallest trees. The redwoods are also very old; some are 2,000 years old. Redwood forests and swiftly running rivers are a part of northern California's environment.

California's Death Valley, the lowest spot in the United States, is also one of the hottest and driest. In Death Valley temperatures have reached 135°F and often there's no rain for years. Death Valley has life forms like pupfish—a fish that can live in mud for the eleven months of the year when streams are dry.

Northern and Southern California

The land in northern California is more like Oregon than like southern California. The land in southern California is more like Mexico than like northern California.

Northern and southern California also differ in lifestyle. Northern Californians accuse southern Californians of being superficial and materialistic—of not being serious and caring only about money and the things money can buy. Southern Californians say that northern Californians are snobby and really are just jealous. Some Californians have proposed that their state be cut in two!

People

California's people come from many different places and cultures. Over one-fourth of California's population is Hispanic. California also has a large Asian population; one-third of all Asian-Americans live in California. It was orig-

inally part of Mexico, and some Hispanics are the descendants of old Californian families. Many others are Mexican-Americans who came more recently. Other Hispanics are from countries in Central and South America. Similarly, Asian-Americans in California first came from one country, China, but now are from many countries—for example, from Japan and the Philippines and, more recently, from Korea, Vietnam, Cambodia, and Laos. People keep moving to California from many parts of the United States and the world. So, California's diverse population is becoming even more diverse!

Puzzle

According to the reading, what is California's main characteristic? (If you know, fill the letters in vertically where indicated and they'll help you with the clues.) To complete the puzzle, you must fill in all the blanks. If you don't know the answer, start with the clues.

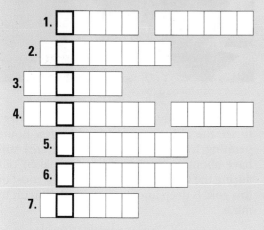

1. It's low, hot and dry
2. One-quarter of California's population
3. Big California business in the 1930s
4. What California symbolizes for many people
5. Tall trees
6. Part of California that Los Angeles is in
7. Country California belonged to

(For the answers, see page 172.)

Scrambled Sentences

The sentences below don't make much sense. That is because each sentence beginning has been combined with the ending of one of the other sentences. Based on the passage, recombine the sentences so that you have six sentences that make sense. Write your new sentences.

1. Southern Californians think that northern Californians are life forms that can survive in mud if necessary.
2. Some Californians were alive 2,000 years ago.
3. Northern Californians think southern Californians are incredibly hot.
4. Pupfish are jealous of the southern Californian lifestyle.
5. Some places in California want to divide the state in two.
6. Some redwoods are only interested in the things money can buy.

Discussion Points

This passage points out that California is diverse—more diverse than people often think.

- What do you think of when you think of California?
- Which aspects discussed here fit with your ideas?
- Which are surprising to you?

The Forty-Niners

In January 1848, a man named James Marshall noticed some flecks of gold in a river in California. Word of Marshall's discovery got around, and by 1849 thousands of people— "forty-niners," as they were called—were on their way to California. Within four short years California's population jumped dramatically and its reputation as a land of opportunity was well established!

The trip to California, over land or by water, was difficult but the rewards were great— at least in the early days. Gold was in the hills, and rivers had eroded the hills. As a result, a miner could get gold simply by panning the rivers—by using a pan to separate the gold in the water from the dirt and rocks.

Often, the most money was made not by miners themselves but by those who had

Tourists pan for gold today. (© *1992 Knott's Berry Farm*)

Today many people visit "gold country" to see the old mines and spend a few hours panning for gold. The hills of the area still have about as much gold as was taken out during the Gold Rush. Unfortunately, most of this gold is deep underground and difficult to mine.

something to sell to the miners. A man named Levi Strauss, who had recently immigrated to the United States, thought he knew just what the miners would buy: He headed for California with canvas for tents.

"Tents!" the miners told him. "We already have tents. You should have brought pants. Pants don't last at all here." A quick thinker, Strauss made his canvas into pants. Miners liked the pants because they were sturdy and lasted. And so Levi's were born.*

*By the 1870s Strauss was making blue jeans much like those today. He'd begun using a strong cotton from Nimes, France called *serge de Nimes* (from "de Nimes" we get the word "denim"). He'd also begun dying the cotton blue and even stitching the pockets with double arcs—the same design you see on Levi's now!

Words
Today "Levi's" can be used to mean "blue jeans." English has other words that, like Levi's, began as names of specific products but now are used in a more general way. Do you know these words?

Kleenex, Xerox, Jello, Q-tip, Scotch tape, Pampers, Walkman

Discussion Point
It's obvious why Levi's were popular with the miners. But what makes Levi's so popular with young people today? Do you like to wear Levi's? Why or why not?

San Francisco

The city of San Francisco was itself a result of the Gold Rush. Forty-niners who went to California by ship passed through San Francisco. Many of them returned to San Francisco—with or without fortunes—to stay. In 1848 San Francisco was a settlement of 200 people. Eight years later it was a city of 50,000.

Earthquakes
On October 17, 1989, millions of Americans turned on their TVs to watch the World Series, the U.S. baseball championship. The Series was between San Francisco and Oakland, its neighbor across the San Francisco Bay. Just as the game was about to start, TV screens went

The Great Earthquake of 1906 destroyed San Francisco.

blank. San Francisco and Oakland had been hit by an earthquake.

Although destructive, this earthquake was insignificant compared to the great quake of 1906.

The 1906 quake struck at 5:00 a.m., jolting people from their beds. (Singer Enrico Caruso, afraid he'd lost his voice, leaned out his hotel window and gave what some say was his best performance ever!) Buildings danced and tumbled, entire streets moved like ocean waves. Fires followed the quakes. Since San Francisco had lost its water supply, little could be done. Finally, after four days, the rains came and the winds changed. Three-fourths of San Francisco had burned down.

A Romantic City, a Liberal City

San Francisco is surrounded on three sides by water. It is famous for its bridges, fog, and foghorns. San Francisco has 40 hills. It is famous for its cable cars, which climb these hills, and for its bright houses that cling to the hills along steep and narrow streets. San Francisco is a wonderful city to explore on foot.

San Francisco also has a reputation as an intellectual, liberal, and slightly crazy city—a city where new and different ideas can be explored.

In the 1950s, San Francisco's North Beach area was a center for "beat poets"; Allen Ginsberg, Lawrence Ferlinghetti, and others gave poetry readings in bookstores and coffee houses.

In the mid-1960s, the Haight-Ashbury district of San Francisco gave rise to hippies (and even to the word "hippie," which comes from the adjective "hip," meaning "aware"). The focus was on rock music, drugs like marijuana and LSD, and love and peace. By 1969 buses of tourists were being driven through Haight-Ashbury.

The college protests that swept America in the late 1960s also began in the San Francisco area—at the University of California, Berkeley, across San Francisco Bay. Always

A cable car

Gay Pride Day in San Francisco

known for academic excellence, in the 60s and 70s Berkeley was even more known for student protest.

Although many movements have faded from the San Francisco scene, the gay rights movement remains strong. San Francisco has one of America's largest gay communities. Gays play an active role in everything from the city's nightlife to its politics.

Visiting San Francisco

Stop in some restaurants. San Francisco's restaurant tradition goes back to forty-niner days. (The first French restaurant, Poulet D'Or, opened in 1849; the miners, unfamiliar with French, called it "Poodle Dog.") Today there are over 4,500 restaurants, serving every cuisine including "California cuisine." California cuisine is based on fresh ingredients and simple but unusual combinations, like grilled tuna with raspberry sauce.

Bookstores in San Francisco are just as varied. Lawrence Ferlinghetti's City Lights Bookstore specializes in poetry. Or, if you prefer mysteries, there's a bookstore with nothing but mysteries—even its bathroom has shelves of mysteries!

To see a genuinely ethnic area, go to Chinatown, the largest Chinese neighborhood outside Asia.

Golden Gate Bridge

Don't leave San Francisco without seeing the structure that has become its symbol—the Golden Gate Bridge. This beautiful orange suspension bridge, which opened in 1937, goes between San Francisco and Marin County to its north.

The bridge was first proposed in 1869 by "Emperor" Norton, a forty-niner who, having lost his money and his mind, had declared himself emperor of the United States. Norton's ideas about an empire may have been crazy, but his idea about a suspension bridge for San Francisco was just ahead of its time. It took twentieth-century technology and the engineering genius of a man named Joseph Strauss to bring the Golden Gate Bridge into existence.

The Golden Gate Bridge

Two Quizzes

A. The facts in some of these sentences are correct, but in others they are not. Correct the sentences that are wrong.

1. Some say Enrico Caruso's greatest performance came when he sang the national anthem before a World Series game.
2. The Poulet D'Or, a restaurant that recently opened in San Francisco, specializes in California cuisine.
3. If you go to a restaurant that serves California cuisine, you are more likely to have fish with berries than steak with potatoes.
4. San Francisco is famous for its cable cars and bridges; in fact, the Golden Gate Bridge has become a symbol of San Francisco.
5. The Golden Gate Bridge was built by an engineering genius who was nicknamed "Emperor" Norton.
6. Over the years, San Francisco has been a center for beat poets, hippies, student protestors, and gays.

B. Replace the italicized words with appropriate nouns or phrases.

1. *It* grew rapidly as a result of the Gold Rush.
2. Two *of them* occurred in 1906 and 1989.
3. There were many *of them* in Haight-Ashbury in the mid-1960s.
4. *That* is what *it* was known for back then, although today it's just known for its academic excellence.

Wine Country

Wine Grapes

California earns more from grapes than from any other crop. Many of the grapes grown are grapes for wine. There are now vineyards and wineries the length of California—down to San Diego, in the very south. But the traditional and most important area for wine lies to the north of San Francisco, in Napa and Sonoma counties.

The wine-making tradition goes back to the 1780s, when Spanish monks planted vine-

Northern California is home to many small wineries.

yards. One of the oldest commercial wineries was started in the 1850s by Count Agoston Haraszthy, a Hungarian who brought to Sonoma many European grape varieties. By the 1880s California wine was winning medals in international competitions. The wine industry flourished until 1920, when the Eighteenth Amendment to the U.S. Constitution was passed.

The Eighteenth Amendment prohibited the making or drinking of alcohol. This amendment caused many problems and was finally repealed in 1933. By that time, the California wine industry had almost been destroyed. The 1960s, however, were the beginning of a wine boom. Growers whose vineyards had survived "Prohibition" were joined by new growers with new techniques. Often these growers came from professions as different as acting or engineering, attracted by their interest in wine and their desire to live in a beautiful place.

Interest in wine and natural beauty also draw many visitors to Napa and Sonoma counties. The area, with its gentle hills covered with vineyards, often reminds people of Mediterranean Europe. Many wineries and fine small restaurants are in old stone buildings. Most wineries give visitors tours and free tastings.

Process of Elimination

The Eighteenth Amendment to the Constitution was repealed by passage of the Twenty-first Amendment. Can you get rid of the "Eighteenth Amendment" here by eliminating all its letters? You can eliminate letters by making a word out of them. Words may contain letters from the two words (e.g., "tent" may be made by using a "t" from each word). You cannot use additional letters, though, and once you have eliminated a letter, you cannot use it again in a new word.

EIGHTEENTH AMENDMENT

Example: dig, amen, tent, theme, then

Silicon Valley

A silicon chip

Santa Clara Valley, south of San Francisco, was famous for its prunes. The valley had acres and acres of prune trees.

In 1939, two young engineers, Bill Hewlett and David Packard, went to work in a garage in the valley. They developed an oscillator, an electronic device.

Today Santa Clara Valley is the most important center of America's computer and electronics industry, and Hewlett-Packard is one of its major firms. More often than not, Santa Clara Valley is referred to by its nickname, Silicon Valley. (Silicon is an element used in making computer chips.)

Silicon Valley developed because there were entrepreneurs with ideas and capitalists who had the money to back them. Companies are more informal than many American workplaces; some almost seem like college campuses. Jogging is a popular lunchtime activity, and engineers are encouraged to spend time thinking about new ideas.

Silicon Valley has changed over the years. Trends today include more attention to computer software, more partnerships with Japanese companies, and consolidation. One key element remains the same: the emphasis on innovation.

Los Angeles

Volleyball at the beach

If, as was said earlier, California is like the United States only more so, then surely Los Angeles is like California only more so. The images most people have when they think of California best fit Los Angeles and the surrounding area.

The Los Angeles area has many beaches, with surfers, volleyball players, and people getting tan. The Los Angeles area is also the center of the movie industry and home to many movie stars. Los Angeles has money and glamour; the Beverly Hills neighborhood, for example, is famous for its mansions and high-priced shops.

One thing that Los Angeles seems *not* to have is a city. Actually, there is a downtown area, but since the 1950s Los Angeles has grown greatly—and it's not grown upward, but grown outward. Los Angeles's "suburbs" are not really suburbs: They not only have houses but also many businesses and offices, and they tend to develop suburbs of their own. So Los Angeles keeps growing, spreading out into farmland and even desert.

Shopping in Beverly Hills

Sprawling suburbs

Rush hour on the freeway in L.A.

love is mixed with a little hate. Los Angeles has four of the five busiest highways in North America. Some days, "rush hour" continues almost unbroken from 7:00 A.M. to 7:00 P.M. Trips, whether to work or to the beach, require planning; one strategy, for example, is to leave for work at four in the morning! Not surprisingly, car phones and, more recently, car fax machines sell well in Los Angeles.

Even if cars don't move quickly in Los Angeles, just about everything else does. Los Angeles is a city of fads and trends. Clubs, restaurants, shops, and styles have been known to appear and disappear overnight or, more precisely, in four quick steps: They are discovered by a few; they are discovered by many; everyone knows about them; they're gone!

This need to be new and different means that whatever you can think of probably exists in L.A. Take juice bars, places that serve fresh juice. One juice bar specializes in weird combinations (for example, apple, garlic, tomato, beet, and ginger all mixed together). Another is also a hair salon; you can drink the same combination that's being used to shampoo your hair!

As distances have increased in Los Angeles, so has the importance of the car. It has often been said that Angelenos have a love affair with the car. Recently, however, that

Angelenos love discovering new restaurants.

Los Angeles's growth is supported by its diverse economy. Los Angeles is a center, not only for entertainment and tourism, but also for manufacturing, business and finance, aerospace, oil, and trade. Its ports now handle more cargo than New York. The growth of trade is largely the result of the strong economies in Asia. Asian companies have also invested heavily in Los Angeles; three-fourths of downtown L.A. is foreign owned, much of it by Japanese.

Los Angeles faces some serious problems. With so much traffic, Los Angeles has the dirtiest air in the United States; all too often the sunshine is hidden by smog. Crime and violence are also major problems. Police say there are at least 500 gangs in Los Angeles. Violence among gang members, who are usually teenagers, has grown with the spread of drugs and drug money. Experts emphasize that the problems must be solved if Los Angeles is to maintain the Southern Californian lifestyle for which it's so famous.

Write

Based on the passage (and on anything else you know about Los Angeles), write a list of things you like about Los Angeles and a list of things you don't like.

Would you want to live in Los Angeles? Write a paragraph explaining why (or why not).

Role Play

Part of the rivalry between Southern and Northern California is a rivalry between Los Angeles and San Francisco. You and a partner will be a Northern Californian from San Francisco and a Southern Californian from Los Angeles. Have a discussion in which you try to convince each other why your area and city are better. (You many want to look back over the readings for information that will help you in the role play.)

Hollywood

Hollywood was once all farmland. By 1910, however, filmmakers began moving there. Southern California's climate was perfect for shooting movies year-round. And the area had settings for just about any movie—it had mountains, desert, and ocean. Soon "Holly-

Mann's Chinese Theater in Hollywood

wood" came to mean "the American film industry."

Today, of the major studios, only Paramount is still in Hollywood. If you go to Hollywood looking for glamour and movie stars, you'll probably be disappointed: Downtown Hollywood looks somewhat run-down, and the stars are nowhere to be found. But then you'll get over your disappointment: Hollywood is no longer what it once was, but it still feels like Hollywood.

In Hollywood you can see two great theaters, where many movies premiered: Pantages Theater and Mann's Chinese. Mann's Chinese (formerly Grauman's Chinese) is famous for its cement courtyard with footprints and handprints of stars who were in—and at!—movies the theater showed. (People say the tradition started when the theater first opened and an actress in the movie being premiered accidently stepped in the still-wet cement.)

Even if you can't see the stars, you can see many things associated with them. Hollywood souvenir shops are filled with autographs, old movie posters, costumes, and stills. Stills are photos of scenes from movies. You can go on a tour, for example, the unusual Grave Line Tour. On this tour, you will travel

in a hearse, the vehicle that usually takes the dead to the grave. The hearse will take you to places where celebrities died.

Hollywood even gives visitors a chance to become stars—on TV game shows. Several shows are based in Hollywood, and visitors can audition, or try out, to be game show participants!

Game

In groups of three, play a vocabulary TV game show. One person is the game show host. He/she chooses 20 words from the passage and writes them down with appropriate definitions. (A dictionary may be used if needed.) The game show host does not show these words to the other two students, who are the game show contestants.

When the host is ready, he or she says the definitions, one at a time. Contestants must think of the words that go with the definitions. They can look at the page in the book. For each definition, the contestant who is first to call out the correct word scores a point. The contestant with the most points at the end wins the game.

Hawaii's History

A volcanic beach on the island of Hawaii

The Hawaiian Islands are volcanic. Volcanoes on the floor of the Pacific grew as a result of eruptions and finally appeared as islands above the ocean's surface. Even today a new Hawaiian island is being formed, although this island won't be visible for another 10,000 years!

The Hawaiian Islands are remote: the nearest land is 2,500 miles away. Yet, as early as 300 A.D., ancient Polynesians, who were skillful navigators, migrated to Hawaii.

Hawaii's first contact with the West wasn't until 1778, when it was "discovered" by English explorer James Cook.

The early 1800s brought great changes. First, Kamehameha, a powerful chief, unified the islands of Hawaii by defeating the other chiefs. He established a monarchy and proved to be a good king. Second, Protestant missionaries from the United States came to Hawaii.

On the positive side, the missionaries applied the alphabet to Hawaiian and soon taught the people to read and write. On the negative side, the missionaries disapproved of Hawaiian culture and did much to discourage it.

There was also a more direct threat to Hawaiian culture: exposure of the population to new diseases. Hawaii's native population dropped from around 300,000 in 1800 to less

Kamehameha (*Choris/Bishop Museum*)

Laborers haul sugarcane on a plantation in the 1890s. (*Bishop Museum*)

than 100,000 in 1860. The most feared disease was leprosy. People with leprosy were taken from their home to the island of Molokai, from which they never returned.

In 1848, the land, which had belonged to the king, was divided up. *Haoles,* the Hawaiian word for foreigners, could now own land, as could Hawaiians. Foreigners soon had large sugarcane plantations.

These plantations required a lot of labor. Workers came from China, and then from Japan, the Philippines, Portugal, and elsewhere. Many workers stayed.

There was growing disagreement between the economically powerful *haoles* and the Hawaiian monarchy. The *haoles* wanted

political reforms and obtained some of them. Then, in 1893, Queen Liliuokalani tried to restore power to the monarchy. The *haoles* overthrew her and set up a government.

The *haoles* were mostly Americans, and they wanted the United States to annex Hawaii. The United States at first refused but soon found itself in need of a military base in the Pacific. In 1900 Hawaii was annexed.

In December 1941, the Japanese surprise attack on the naval base at Pearl Harbor, Hawaii brought the United States into World War II.

In 1959, Hawaii was made the 50th state. Just as important, the first jet landed in Hawaii. With quicker, cheaper travel, Hawaii's tourist industry boomed.

Queen Liliukalani (*Waverly, London, England. Issued by J. Gonsalves Bishop Museum*)

Answer
1. How were the Hawaiian Islands formed?
2. Where did the native Hawaiian people originally come from?
3. Who was the first European to visit Hawaii?
4. What did Kamehameha accomplish?
5. What countries did people move to Hawaii from in the nineteenth century?
6. Where did the missionaries come from? What were some effects of their presence in Hawaii?
7. What happened to Queen Liliukalani?
8. What were two important events for Hawaii in 1959?

Hawaii Today

Honolulu

Economy

Today tourism accounts for 30 percent of Hawaii's income—a figure that won't surprise anyone who has been to crowded Waikiki beach! Tourists come from around the world but especially from the U.S. mainland and Japan.

Hawaii's agricultural products include sugar, pineapple, and macadamia nuts. (The macadamia nut industry had a slow start since these nuts are very hard and a more effective nutcracker had to be developed!) Hawaii even produces coffee and, since 1980, a highly praised pineapple wine.

People

Hawaii's people today are from many groups— Japanese, American, Chinese, and Filipinos. Less than one percent of the population is pure Hawaiian, but many people have some

Waikiki Beach is a popular place with tourists.

Hawaiians celebrate their culture.

Hawaiian blood. Today one of every two marriages is between people of different groups.

Hawaiian culture reflects this ethnic mix. Hawaii has been described as a place where East meets West. It has also been described as a mixture of U.S. culture and its own island culture, with "island culture" meaning the combination that has developed from all the groups that settled there.

Language

Not surprisingly, in one-fourth of Hawaii's homes, the main language spoken is something other than English. And everybody's everyday speech contains some words from all the languages spoken. Hawaiian is especially important. For example, Hawaiian *aloha* is just as common as *hello*, Hawaiian *mahalo* just as common as *thank you*. In giving directions, people often use the Hawaiian *mauka* (toward the mountains) and *makai* (toward the sea). Hawaiian words have many vowels and repeated syllables. They can be quite long; for example there is a small fish called a *humuhumunukunukuapuaa*.

Pidgin is also spoken in Hawaii. It began in the nineteenth century, as a kind of combination of languages that enabled workers from different countries to communicate. Modern pidgin is more like slang and is used especially by teenagers. Common phrases include *tanks brah* (from "thanks, brother") for

"thanks" and *an' den?* (from "and then?") for "what else happened?" or "so what?" It's possible to have entire conversations in pidgin.

Surfing

When James Cook reached Hawaii in 1778, he was astonished to see people on boards riding the waves. Although surfing was unknown in the West, the thrill was immediately obvious to Cook. Watching one surfer, he wrote, "I could not help concluding this man felt the most supreme pleasure." Surfing had come from ancient Polynesia and for centuries had been practiced as an art and a sport, especially by the royalty.

The missionaries thought the surfers were insufficiently dressed. As a result of their influence, surfing nearly died out.

In the end, far from dying, surfing spread around the world. Surfing became *really* popular once light boards were developed. (Traditional surfboards weighed about 150 pounds!)

Hawaii has some of the world's best surfing. Serious surfers go to Hawaii in winter to catch the dangerous 25-foot high waves off the beaches of Oahu.

A surfer in action

Words: *Da kine*

A phrase often heard in pidgin is *da kine*. *Da kine* is similar to—but, Hawaiians say, more expressive than—the English *whatchamacallit*. English speakers sometimes use *whatchamacallit* when they can't think of a word but know the listener will know what they have in mind (e.g., "Can you hand me the what-chamacallit?").

Does your language have a word equivalent to *da kine?* What would you say in a situation like the one described above?

Discussion Points

- Is there any surfing in your country? Have you ever surfed? If so, what was it like? If not, do you think you'd like to? Why or why not? What is your favorite water sport?
- Hawaii's culture is described as being a real mix of the cultures of the different people who settled there. What things about Hawaii do you think helped make this mixture of cultures possible? Have you been to any places that you thought had a real mix of cultures? If so, describe them.

Glossary

academic related to school and studies

acre a measure of land equal to about 4,000 square meters

annex to take possession of something (e.g., of a territory)

astonished very surprised

autograph the signature of a famous person

aware of knowing about or realizing something

blank empty, with nothing on it

cable car a car that is moved along a rail by means of a wire up above or below

capitalist a person who has money for use in financing businesses

cement a material that becomes hard when dry and is used for sidewalks, buildings, etc.

championship game(s) played to decide who is champion

consolidation a coming together into one, e.g., of two or more businesses

diverse of all different kinds

entrepreneur someone who organizes and runs a business and who is willing to take the necessary risks

erode to wear away

fad a fashion, interest, or enthusiasm that is not likely to last

fax a machine that sends printed material electronically

fleck a tiny piece

flourish to grow and prosper

fog a fine mist suspended in the air and difficult to see through

foghorn a horn to give ships warning in the fog

fortune a great deal of money

game show a TV program where contestants try to win prizes

gang a group of people associating together, especially young people who engage in activities that are not accepted or that are against the law

glamour an exciting attractiveness

give rise to to allow the growth of

innovation change, introduction of things that are new

insignificant not important

intellectual (*n*) a person who likes to read, think about things, explore ideas, etc.

invest to put money into a business, etc., in hopes of making a profit

jogging slow running for exercise

last (*v*) to continue on

leprosy a disease characterized by sores on the skin and loss of feeling

liberal having a broad mind and being tolerant, being in favor of progress

LSD a hallucinogenic drug, which may cause people to see things that aren't there

maintain to keep

missionary someone doing religious work and/or trying to convert people, especially in a foreign country

monarchy a government run by a king or queen

mystery a story in which a crime is described and treated as a puzzle to be solved

navigator someone who steers a boat, especially for a long distance

negative not good

overthrow to bring down a government

pineapple a sweet, juicy fruit with an oval shape and stiff leaves at the top

positive favorable; good

premiere the first showing of a movie

propose to suggest

reform (*n*) change that is meant to bring improvements

repeal of laws, to put an end to

run-down no longer in good condition

rush hour the time when traffic is heavy because people are coming from or going to work

screen the surface on which a movie is shown

slang words and phrases that are used informally, often only for a period of time

smog fog mixed with smoke and chemical fumes

suburb a neighborhood that is right outside a city and that mainly has houses

surf (*v*) to ride the waves on a board

threat a danger

trendy following the latest fashion or style

tumble to fall

unify to bring together into one

variety a kind; different kinds

vineyard land where grapes are grown

visible able to be seen

volleyball a game in which two teams hit a ball over a net

Answer Key

New England

Words (page 20)
1. g 2. b 3. f 4. e 5. a 6. d 7. c

A Yankee Replies (page 20)
New England Yankee:
Yep. I know where

Complete (page 21)
Salem, judge, witch, curse, *The House of the Seven Gables,* Walden, civil disobedience, taxes

Word Search (page 23)

True or False (page 27)
1. F 2. F 3. T 4. T 5. F

New York City

Puzzle (page 36)

```
W O R L D T R A D E
A     U         A
L O W T       N Y S E
L     C     H   T
S O U T H   E
T     R     L
R     I N D I A N S
E     N     C
E     K   B O A T
T R E E   P     W
      T   T     I
  F I S H   E   N
          R
```

Scrambled Sentences (page 40)
1. Before the bohemians arrived, the Village was mainly an Italian and Irish neighborhood.
2. East Sixth Street has many Indian restaurants that are both good and cheap.
3. The New York "club scene" changes very rapidly.

Mid-Atlantic Region

Complete (page 54)
nation, confederation, Philadelphia, Constitution

Puzzle (page 56)
TO HAVE FUN

The South

Puzzle (page 68)
In 1860, Abraham Lincoln was elected.

Riddle (page 72)
a sieve

Answer (page 72)
1. a. Once or twice a night; chimneys
   b. to suppose
   c. quietly, smoothly, awfully

Adjectives (page 74)
1. f 2. g 3. d 4. a 5. b 6. e 7. c

Adjectives (page 89)
1. d 2. b 3. e 4. f 5. c 6. a 7. g

The Midwest

Hidden Words (page 90)
1. a. FORD
   b. AFFORDABLE
2. a. PORT
   b. IMPORT
3. a. FLAT
   b. INFLATION

Word Search (page 92)

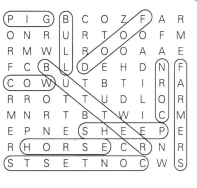

Words:
bull   horse   pig   sheep   corn
butter   cow   food   farmers   contests

Scrambled Words (page 92)
1. b. tornado   2. c. blizzard   3. a. thunderstorm

The Southwest

Puzzle   (page 102)
1. sod
2. boomers
3. moisture
4. Depression
5. grasshoppers
6. California

Oklahoma's nickname: The **Sooner** State

Puzzle   (page 110)
1. sh**o**t
2. divorce
3. **shirt**

Note: to "lose your shirt" means to lose a large amount gambling.

The Rocky Mountain Region

Nouns and Verbs   (page 128)
1.b. lie   2.d tire   3.c. match   4.a. sink   5.e. park

A Giant Crossword Puzzle   (page 131)

The Pacific Northwest and Alaska

Words   (page 135)
sunny   Sunday   sunbathe   sunburn
sunlight   sunrise   sunset   sunny-side up

Match   (page 139)
1. f   2. d   3. e   4. a   5. b   6. c

True or False   (page 139)
1. T   2. F   3. F   4. T   5. F   6.F

California and Hawaii

Puzzle   (page 155)
1. Death Valley
2. Hispanic
3. movies
4. American Dream
5. redwoods
6. southern
7. Mexico

California is: **Diverse**